Trauma, Guilt and

CW00818750

Trauma, Guilt and Reparation identifies the emotional barriers faced by people who have experienced severe trauma, as well as the emergence of reparative processes which pave the way from impasse to development.

The book explores the issue of trauma with particular reference to issues of reparation and guilt. Referencing the original work of Klein and others, it examines how feelings of persistent guilt work to foil attempts at reparation, locking trauma deep within the psyche. It provides a theoretical understanding of the interplay between feelings of neediness with those of fear, wrath, shame and guilt, and offers a route for patients to experience the mourning and forgiveness necessary to come to terms with their own trauma. The book includes a Foreword by John Steiner.

Illustrated by clinical examples throughout, it is written by an author whose empathy and experience make him an expert in the field. The book will be of great interest to psychotherapists, social workers and any professional working with traumatised individuals.

Heinz Weiss, M.D., is the Head of the Department of Psychosomatic Medicine at the Robert Bosch Hospital in Stuttgart. He is also the head of the Medical Division and member of the directorate of the Sigmund-Freud-Institute, Frankfurt/Main, and Chair of the Education Section of *The International Journal of Psychoanalysis*.

'Despite the fact that in recent decades the importance of trauma in the production of adult pathology has been rediscovered, there are few works that fall into the clinic to show in detail the specific link between suffering and original trauma. Weiss's book does it; he questions the quality of the trauma, from the emotional to the violent, and the question arises of how it is possible to repair the damage and what the relationship between the new object, the analyst, and the permanence of the internalized traumatic experience can be. This is an in-depth and well-documented study with rich and detailed clinical cases. In particular, the author studies the problem of reparation, mourning resentment, revenge, shame and finally of gratitude. A book that invites us to think about a complex but essential theoretical and clinical theme in psychoanalytic treatment.'

–**Franco de Masi**, Training and Supervising Analyst of the Italian
Psychoanalytical Society and former President of Centro
Milanese di Psicoanalisi and Secretary of the
Training Milanese Institute

'Severely disturbed and traumatized patients present analysts and therapists with some of the most complex and difficult challenges in contemporary clinical practice. Agonizing guilt, long lasting grievance, hatred and rage complicate and threaten to derail the reparative and mourning processes needed for recovery. Based on the author's extensive clinical experience, Trauma, Guilt and Reparation offers readers a thoughtful, richly illustrated, comprehensive approach to these problems and serves to help advance analytic understanding and practice.'

–**Howard B. Levine**, MD, Editor-in-Chief,
The Routledge W. R. Bion Studies Series

Trauma, Guilt and Reparation

The Path from Impasse to Development

Heinz Weiss

Translated by
Dr Ursula Haug

 Routledge
Taylor & Francis Group

LONDON AND NEW YORK

First published in English 2020
by Routledge
2 Park Square, Milton Park, Abingdon, Oxon OX14 4RN

and by Routledge
52 Vanderbilt Avenue, New York, NY 10017

Routledge is an imprint of the Taylor & Francis Group, an informa business

English edition © 2020 Heinz Weiss
Translated by Dr Ursula Haug

© Klett-Cotta – J.G. Cotta'sche Buchlandlung Nachfolger GmbH,
Stuttgart

British Library Cataloguing-in-Publication Data
A catalogue record for this book is available from the British Library

Library of Congress Cataloging-in-Publication Data
Names: Weiss, Heinz, 1955- author.
Title: Trauma, guilt and reparation : the path from impasse to
development / Heinz Weiss ; translated by Dr. Ursula Haug.
Other titles: Trauma, Schuldgefühl und Wiedergutmachung. English
Description: Abingdon, Oxon ; New York, NY : Routledge, 2020. |
Includes bibliographical references and index. |
Identifiers: LCCN 2019036865 | ISBN 9780367185381 (hardback) |
ISBN 9780367185411 (paperback) | ISBN 9780429196768 (ebook)
Subjects: LCSH: Psychic trauma. | Guilt. | Reparation (Psychoanalysis)
Classification: LCC BF175.5.P75 W37513 2020 | DDC 155.9/3--dc23
LC record available at https://lccn.loc.gov/2019036865

ISBN: 978-0-367-18538-1 (hbk)
ISBN: 978-0-367-18541-1 (pbk)
ISBN: 978-0-429-19676-8 (ebk)

Typeset in Times New Roman
by Taylor & Francis Books

To Claudia Frank

Contents

Foreword

John Steiner

This is an important and interesting book that offers a new slant on the problem of how to help severely disturbed and traumatised patients. These patients have often been the victims of adverse circumstances including neglect, violence and sexual abuse and the wrongs done to them have left a sense of injury and hurt that profoundly affects both the world view of the victim and those who are called in to help.

Confronting psychotic and borderline patients in everyday practice means that you cannot avoid facing disturbing facts of life; and the terrible cruelty that some of our patients have suffered means that we cannot help but feel concerned on their behalf. We empathise with the patient's suffering and, of course, we blame those who failed to offer the secure start to life that is needed for healthy development. However, as we listen to our patients, a paradoxical situation commonly emerges in which the patients come to blame themselves and, both consciously or unconsciously, are obliged to grapple with guilt and shame which is often associated with the trauma itself.

Of course, sometimes the victim played a role in instituting or prolonging the trauma, but even those who seem to be completely innocent targets of abuse are left with a problematic relationship with their internal objects which can be extremely complex and difficult to disentangle in therapy. They are confronted with figures from their earliest years who inflicted damaging experiences onto them, but who themselves were also damaged. The patients feel hatred and are often drawn into phantasies and actions driven by revenge which sometimes inflict further damage and a vicious cycle, in which the victim hates the perpetrator and vice versa, becomes difficult to interrupt.

These issues form the central core of this important book in which Heinz Weiss explores the complex relationships that give rise to guilt and their relation to reparation and gratitude. What he shows, in admirable detail and sensitivity, is that even in severely traumatised patients, the vicious cycle of trauma leading to revenge and persecution can be broken as the patient begins to accept his own part in the creation of the persecuting situation. Only when the patient's own guilt is faced can moves begin in the direction of restoring his internal objects and creating a healthier internal environment which can enable further development. The central concept in these moves is that of making reparation and Weiss links this first to the acknowledgement of guilt and then to the emergence of gratitude.

Heinz Weiss is extremely well equipped to write a book of such sensitivity and breadth. In addition to his clinical experience in the course of conduction psychoanalysis, even with patients as difficult as those he describes, he directs a model day-hospital service in which psychoanalytical therapy, both group and individual, are offered to borderline and other severely disturbed patients. This gives him both a broad understanding on the one hand and a deep one on the other and enables him to provide the reader with an outstanding survey of this fascinating area of mental life.

It is important to stress that this approach in no way diminishes the often-devastating effects of external trauma and it is remarkable that the analysis of guilt, reparation, forgiveness and gratitude can prove to be a productive area to explore in analysis, and one which patients are often grateful for. Those analysts who side with the patient's grievance in their protest at what has been done can make the patient feel that, rather than find understanding, they have manipulated the analyst to collude with a partial version of the truth of what happened to them and how they have reacted to it.

It is the link between reparation and gratitude that is one of the most original aspects of the author's work and he rightly points out that gratitude is a topic that has not been sufficiently explored in the past. Of course, if trauma has been severe, the patient often feels he has not received much to be grateful for and he is more likely to respond with grievance and hatred. However, teasing out the complex relationships enables the analyst to understand the guilt that so commonly lies beneath the hatred and is so important because it can harness the patient's capacity to love and to forgive. First, the hatred has to be experienced and analysed in the transference, and then, when the damage the hatred has done emerges more clearly, the guilt can be faced and, paradoxically, this lessens as the damage done gives rise to sorrow and regret. These moves can lead to reparation being embarked on and the relationship with the traumatising object is then less black and white so that both good and bad elements come to be recognised.

One of the significant conclusions that Heinz Weiss comes to is that both reparation and gratitude require an acknowledgement of separateness between self and object. It involves a recognition that the object contains good things from which we have received benefit and a critical issue that remains unanswered is why this should sometimes be so unbearable that it provokes envy and a wish to destroy the goodness of the object, while at other times it can be tolerated and then permits feelings of gratitude to emerge. It all hinges on the capacity to tolerate reality, both the cruel reality of the external world that provokes such violent reactions in us, but also the equally complex reality of inner wishes and phantasies.

Heinz Weiss admits we are far from fully understanding what makes it possible to tolerate reality and especially guilt. He suggests that one factor might be the capacity to recognise transience, which he finds impressive in those patients who are able to be in touch with gratitude. If we have omnipotently created a phantasy of endless benevolence, gratitude loses its relevance, while if we are in touch with something good and know that we can only enjoy for a short time, its value is enhanced.

The theme of transience connects with important previous work Heinz Weiss has done on the experience of the passage of time (Weiss 2009). He has shown how the recognition that time passes is an essential aspect of reality which involves facing our mortality and the inevitability that 'all good things come to an end', including life itself (Money-Kyrle, 1968). If we cannot accept our mortality then it is impossible to work through the task of mourning which is so essential to development. It is perhaps the acceptance of the reality of the passage of time that is the most important factor in enabling envy to give way to gratitude. The envious struggle to exact revenge and to reverse traumata done to us can then sometimes be relinquished when it is recognised that it is too late and no longer worth the trouble to try to undo rather than accept the damage done. We can then resign ourselves to what life we have left to enjoy and be grateful for what we have.

Of course, the importance of reparation is that bad objects become less bad as they are placed in context and their complexities are better understood. In this way good objects are repaired and the internal world, in particular the severe super-ego figures, become less terrifying so that guilt also lessens. However, it is also important to remember that when the object is seen more realistically it is not only goodness that emerges more realistically. Reparation leads to a lessening of distortions including those of idealisation of good objects so that bad objects that really did inflict trauma can be seen more realistically as bad and, paradoxically, this enables good objects and the good aspects of complex objects to be loved in a deeper way. We do not then pretend that trauma did not occur and we are ready more wholeheartedly to hate the bad things that happened and to love the good things. As splitting lessens, both the love and hatred are directed to the same object and this provides some of the most painful and difficult aspects of our relationships that we have to learn to live with. It is here that gratitude for the good experience can emerge alongside residual disappointments and resentments that bad things also happened.

Heinz Weiss explores these themes in great depth and while theoretically informed and sophisticated his understanding is firmly based in his clinical work. Because he presents detailed material from his clinical practice, the reader can study the case material and decide for himself if he agrees with the theoretical points that emerge. I think this book might be the end of simplistic accounts of serious trauma in which either internal or external factors are all that are considered. What emerges is the complex way that trauma and the damage it leaves behind interferes with the capacity for making reparation and hence for releasing gratitude.

References

Money-Kyrle, R. (1971). The aim of psycho-analysis. *Int. J. Psycho-anal.*, 52, 103–106, Reprinted in *The Collected Papers of Roger Money-Kyrle*, 442–449 (1978). Perthshire: Clunie Press.

Weiss, H. (2009). *Das Labyrinth der Borderline-Kommunikation. Klinische Zugänge zum Erleben von Raum und Zeit* [*The Labyrinth of Borderline-Communication. How to Access Clinically the Experience of Space and Time*]. Stuttgart: Klett-Cotta.

Preface and acknowledgements

As I look back on my exploration of *The Labyrinth of Borderline Communication* (Weiss 2009), I notice that I did not pay enough attention to a central problem area for these patients, which is the difficulty they have in coming to terms with their traumatic past and how to re-enliven the damaged objects of their internal world. Yet it is this failure in their effort of reparation and renewal which leads to so many dead ends and cycles of repetition in the life of these patients: for the limited internal space they have available, for the difficulty in symbolising emotional experiences, their tendency to get involved in pathological relationship patterns, the agonising internal emptiness which attacks them time and again, their panic-stricken anxiety about loss, but also of closeness, which is experienced as threatening, and finally, the attraction of timeless, psychic retreats, which appear to offer a certain degree of security, but block development and psychic change in the long run.

All these phenomena can be understood as an expression of damaging and damaged internal figures, whose restoration is exceedingly difficult. In a series of seminars and conferences in recent years on the significance of guilt feelings in early traumatised patients, I became increasingly aware of the role of failed processes of reparation. It is this failure which maintains the cycle of retaliation, the repetition compulsion and the self-punishment. The hope that psychoanalytic treatment holds out is that the damaged capacity for reparation can be, at least in part, regained. This confronts patient and analyst alike with the painful insight that the damages of the past cannot be undone and psychological scars will remain, but the patients can also learn to live better despite and with their handicap.

This book examines the anatomy of failed and successful reparation processes in the face of early trauma and guilt. It would not have been possible to write without the trust of my patients, to whom I am grateful for the insights they gave to me during the course of their long treatments.

A special thank you goes to my friend and psychoanalytic comrade, Claudia Frank, to whom this book is dedicated. She has accompanied my explorations for more than three decades and has sharpened my perception of the primitive and mature processes of reparation through her pioneering work on Melanie Klein's early child analyses.

Her seminal work on symbol formation and the aesthetic theory of psychoanalysis (Frank 2002; 2006; 2013; 2015b, c; 2017) would not have been possible without the concept of reparation. She has written several seminal papers on symbol formation and the psychoanalytic theory of aesthetics in which the concept of reparation plays a prominent role. Furthermore, she has taken up important clinical questions (Frank 2003a, b; 2015a) and has significantly contributed to the close contact with London psychoanalysts with whom our shared investigations were generated.

Among these colleagues I would like to mention particularly John Steiner, Hanna Segal and Edna O'Shaughnessy. With their examinations of envy and gratitude, symbolisation and artistic creativity, as well as the topography of psychic retreats, they have provided the basis for the concept of reparation developed here. John Steiner supervised several of the treatments presented in this book over many years. Without the personal communication with him, the research seminars he undertook in our department and participation in his postgraduate seminar, many of the ideas developed here would not have emerged. Furthermore, he let me see Melanie Klein's lectures on treatment technique, which were not yet published when this book was prepared. I am grateful to Hanna Segal for the possibility to discuss borderline and psychotic cases with her, which have found their way into this book.

I am also grateful to numerous colleagues for their support and comments, among them Anja Kidess, Esther Horn and other members of staff in the Department of Psychosomatic Medicine of the Robert Bosch Hospital in Stuttgart. The daily exchange of clinical experiences as well as the seminars with students and practising colleagues run together with Claudia Frank has contributed in equal measure to the development of my thinking.

Through my involvement with the Sigmund-Freud Institute in Frankfurt, I became familiar with wider aspects of traumatic experiences including the consequences of migration, of being a refugee, of being forced to leave one's country in the context of current social and political developments. I would like to thank my co-workers in the directorate, Vera King and Patrick Meurs, for the trusting co-operation as well as the Robert Bosch Foundation, the Heidehof Foundation and the Robert Bosch Hospital for the manifold support of our work.

Further thanks go to Marianne Leuzinger-Bohleber and Werner Bohleber (Frankfurt a. M.), Franco De Masi (Milano), David Taylor (London), Tuelay Özbek (Berlin) and Martin Teising (Berlin) for their comments on different chapters of the book.

Esther Horn (Stuttgart) read through the whole text and drew my attention to and discussed various points of importance with me. In addition, she translated the foreword by John Steiner for the German edition of this book. Her collegial companionship and her co-operation were of great importance in the preparation of this book.

I thank Leonard Weiss (Munich) for indicating the many links of psychoanalytic concepts with philosophical traditions, resulting in convergences as well as in differences. A special thank you to my wife, Carina Weiss, who, as a classical archaeologist, widened my perception of the antique sources of our modern ideas. I could discuss many of the ideas, which have become part of this book with her. Furthermore, most of the images in this book were prepared by her.

My thanks go also to Russell George (Routledge, London) and Heinz Beyer (Klett-Cotta, Stuttgart) for our long-lasting and trustful co-operation and support, which made the publication of this book possible.

Finally, I wish to thank my friend and psychoanalytic colleague, Ursula Haug (London), for her translation of this book and her empathic understanding of my ideas.

Stuttgart, Frankfurt
March 2019
Heinz Weiss

Chapter 1

Trauma, guilt and reparation

A psychoanalytic paradigm

It is a common and yet paradoxical phenomenon that people who have been exposed to traumatic experiences are frequently plagued by agonising guilt. Internal and external reality get mixed up in their phantasy, and the more external reality is dominated by the internal phantasy world, the more people experience themselves drawn into complex dilemmas. The consequences of these enmeshments can be manifold. They can be directed towards the self or the person's own body, may lead to long-lasting feelings of grievance and resentment, can generate bizarre physical symptoms or invite collusion with cruel objects, who are turned into 'guardians' and powerful figures. What all these scenarios have in common is that psychic development is impeded and the resulting repetition compulsion makes them relatively resistant to change (Freud 1914g; 1920g).

In this book, I shall argue that the repetition compulsion can only be overcome when processes of reparation gradually emerge to re-balance and limit the damage in the internal world. In this context, reparation refers less to the external situation, which in most cases is irretrievably irreparable, but to the destructive and self-destructive forces which emanate from it. In this sense, reparation is different from repair, concrete restoration or a simple undoing of what has happened. It is not about straightforward remedial work, compensation or revenge. The aim is to achieve an *acknowledgement of loss*, which means recognising that the damage has been done and things can never be as they were before.

In this way, reparation is a *symbolic process*, which is never quite finished. As well as the recognition of loss, a capacity to deal with feelings of guilt is required, regardless of whether they are located in the self or in the other.

In his or her phantasy, the child often feels responsible for the state of his objects and the damage done to them. In this case, submission can protect from persecutory anxiety, as hatred of those figures would make them appear even more threatening. Another constellation could be that destructive and self-destructive impulses are relocated outside, so that the individual no longer feels threatened by them internally. Yet, in one way or another, some kind of 'complicity' develops, which makes it almost impossible to distinguish reality from unconscious phantasy, and makes it difficult to deal with feelings of mourning and guilt.

However, the capacity to differentiate between internal and external reality, between present and past, are essential prerequisites in regaining the internal space which in itself facilitates the working through of mourning and guilt (see Kogan 2007). Because, where guilt feelings have either assumed a persecutory quality or are not accessible at all, there is no possibility of reparation.

It is the intention of this book to explore how processes of reparation can get stuck and under which conditions they can be re-activated by closely examining difficult treatment situations, i.e. by exploring processes which re-establish internal space and enable '*remembering with emotion and meaning*' (O'Shaughnessy 1989; Weiss 2009). Because trauma knows neither time nor place, it is everywhere and nowhere. It overwhelms the present with a past that never ended and fails to have a future because it is an endless repetition of the same. The thesis put forward here is that the individual can only re-find his or her history when internal processes of reparation begin to emerge.

Developments in the psychoanalytic concept of trauma

More than any other body of theories, psychoanalysis has never regarded traumatic experiences as only the consequence of external events, but conceptualised them as an *interplay of internal and external realities*. To what extent a situation is experienced as traumatic does not solely depend on external factors, but on its impact on internal reality. And conversely, the internal world of the individual is fundamentally influenced by the experiences of his early relationships. What looks from one point of view as being overwhelmed by an overpowering reality is experienced from another perspective like an 'explosion' of an unconscious phantasy (Britton 2005).

Psychoanalysis has oscillated between exploring both poles and examining the axes which connect them (see Fenichel 1945). In his paper 'Inhibitions, symptoms and anxiety' Freud (1926d, p. 166) characterises the state that is described as 'traumatic' as an experience of impotence and helplessness. Using the example of early object loss, he shows that this loss extends to external objects just as well as to the idea of the internal object relationship and goes on to say that it is the loss of the *internal relationship* which leads to the helplessness he described.

Helplessness engenders anxiety and pain long before other feelings, such as mourning, gradually emerge, i.e. before reality can be recognised and paralysing impotence can be overcome (ibid. pp. 169–171). In this context, impotence not only refers to a state of being overwhelmed by internal and external dangers but also to being overwhelmed by the protective measures available to deal with this helplessness.

In this way there is a continuity between Freud's early work (Freud & Breuer 1895d, pp. 2–16; 1896a, pp. 151–152; 1896b, pp. 162–163), where he highlighted the topic of traumatic sexual experiences, going on to the important role of unconscious phantasy which he explored after abandoning the 'seduction theory'[1], up to his late work (Freud 1920g; 1926d) where he investigated the connection between the breakdown of the 'stimulus barrier' and the onset of the repetition compulsion (see Garland 1998, pp. 9–31).

In abandoning the 'seduction theory', Freud initially turned away from the idea that neurotic illness was invariably brought about by traumatic childhood experiences. With the onset of his own self-analysis, he delved into the significance of unconscious phantasies. The regularly produced 'memories' his patients brought during treatment did no longer seem to correspond to historic reality. In part, they turned out to be retrospectively distorted transformations. He came to 'a certain insight that there are no indications of reality in the unconscious, so that one cannot distinguish between truth and fiction that is cathected with affect' (Freud 1950a [1897], p. 264). But the 'general collapse of all values' (ibid. p. 266) was not as radical as he initially assumed in September 1897.[2]

Freud had already apportioned phantasy a decisive role in the working through of traumatic experiences. In a letter to his colleague and friend Wilhelm Fließ of 11th January 1897, he suggested that the development of neurotic or psychotic symptoms depended on the *time of impact* of the traumatic experience on the immature psychic organisation of the child (Freud 1950a, pp. 221–223) and in 'Manuscript M' from May of the same year (ibid. pp. 246–248) he distinguishes different types of transformation and distortion by subsequent phantasy formation. At the same time, he developed the concept of 'afterwardness' *(Nachträglichkeit)* (Freud 1896a, p. 153; 1899a; 1909b; 1918b, pp. 45, 54; 1925a; 1937d; 1950a, pp. 278–282; see Eickhoff 2005) and thus created for the first time an idea that certain experiences come into effect *not at the time of their happening* but only *at a later time,* for instance, when going through a vulnerable phase of psychic development (see Baranger et al. 1988; Birksted-Breen 2003).

Even though the discovery of the unconscious brought the research into the unknown internal world into the foreground, Freud never disregarded the pathogenic significance of constitutional and external factors in psychic development. With the introduction of the 'repetition compulsion' (Freud 1914g) and the re-organisation of his drive theory, he again returned to the role of traumatic experiences in 1920. In his view, they break through the 'stimulus barrier', whose maintenance is essential for psychic balance. As they cannot be assimilated by the immature psyche, they result in repetitive cycles, the repetition compulsion, whose origin Freud now assumes to be 'beyond the pleasure principle'.

In the same paper, Freud (1920g) examines the conditions in which a breakdown of psychic organisation occurs. Again, he distinguishes between *internal* and *external defences against danger*. In a speculative leap, he describes the function of a 'cortical layer' which is supposed to protect the psyche from excessive excitement. This is assumed to be differentiated into an *external* and *internal* layer. The former has the task of selectively checking the external world through the sense organs and protecting the psyche from external overstimulation. The latter aims at binding and neutralising the excitation from internal drive stimulation. For the latter task, dreams are of decisive significance because, as Freud explains in advance of his 'signal theory' of anxiety (Freud 1926d), which he is yet to develop, they 'are endeavouring to master the stimulus retrospectively, by developing the anxiety whose omission was the cause of the traumatic neurosis.' (Freud 1920g, p. 31). This 'binding' of psychic energy through dreams is, according to Freud, a separate phenomenon, that goes beyond the characteristic wish fulfilment. It touches on the *more primary function of dreaming,* before the dominance of the pleasure principle, as shown, for instance, in those dreams 'which bring to memory the psychical traumas of childhood' (ibid. p. 32).

This point of view seems close to contemporary thinking considering, for instance, Wilfred Bion's (1962 pp. 17–22) notion of the function of a 'contact barrier'. Bion describes the 'contact barrier' as a 'semi-permeable membrane', which in the course of psychic development enables the distinction of internal and external reality and to separate the functions of the conscious and unconscious. It protects the psyche from being overwhelmed by sensory perceptions and at the same time preserves the perception of the external world from the danger of being swamped by internal excitation. Exactly at this interface, which serves as a *connection as well as a boundary*, Bion places the development of primary symbolic elements in the form of 'dream thoughts'.

There are parallels to actual neuro-physiological research, although not easily transferable for epistemological reasons, in which structural changes and disturbances in the excitation process of the central nervous system in traumatised patients could be shown (Schore 2001; van der Kolk 2003; Teicher et al. 2003; Gabbard et al. 2006; McCrory et al. 2011). Such 'scars' in the processing of signals in the central nervous system were linked to changes in the regulation of affect and pain in borderline patients (Schmahl et al. 2006; Ducasse et al. 2014; Simons et al. 2014), but also linked to processes of memory consolidation (Leuzinger-Bohleber 2015; Leuzinger-Bohleber & Pfeifer 2015).

From a psychoanalytic point of view, the equivalent of the function of the 'contact barrier' is the continuous exchange between internal and external reality, i.e. a balance of projective and introjective processes, which facilitates a gradually growing complexity and symbolisation of emotional experiences. As perception is linked to feelings and fantasies, it acquires *meaning,* in comparing internal states with sensory perceptions they take on *reality* and *weight.*

Looking at it in terms of developmental psychology, this balance of projective and introjective processes will be established through the earliest interactions of the infantile psyche in the parental setting. If the 'contact barrier' is understood as an *intersubjective phenomenon* that enables as well as limits exchange (Teising 2005), traumatic experiences become understandable as disturbances in early relationships. It does make a difference whether a child grows up in an atmosphere of diffuse anxiety and latent violence, looks into the eyes of a depressive mother, is surrounded by nameless guilt or whether the child is accepted with his loving and hateful sides, or experiences rejection or falls into an unfathomable emptiness.

This elementary and potentially traumatising effect of the primary communication between parent and child was emphasised by Sándor Ferenczi early on. Based on observations in the treatment of regressed patients, he examined the consequences of transgressions, denial and dishonesty on the infantile psyche in his papers 'Child-analysis in the analysis of adults' (1931) and 'Confusion of the tongues between the adults and the child' (1949). He came to regard the role of pathological identification, the introjection of guilt feelings as well as splitting-processes, aimed at avoiding feelings of helplessness and confusion, as particularly long lasting. He described the specifics of such splitting as regression to a state of 'pre-traumatic bliss', while another part of the personality experiences a 'traumatic progression' with the development of intellectual prematurity, which remains cut off from the rest of emotional development (Ferenczi 1949, p. 228).

Following on from Ferenczi, it was in particular Michael Balint (1968; 1969) and Donald W. Winnicott (1960a) who emphasised the role of a good enough primary relationship in a holding environment. A lack of appropriate receptive capacity in the parents promotes the development of 'ego-distortions' in the form of a 'false self' based on compliance (Winnicott 1960b). However, at the same time, Winnicott emphasised that from a psychoanalytic point of view there is 'no trauma (...) outside of the individual's omnipotence' adding that interpretations promoting psychic change are those 'that can be made in terms of projection' (1960a, p. 586).

Numerous authors have pointed out the significance of cumulative and sequential emotional traumatisation (Khan 1964; Keilson 1979; Grubrich-Simitis 1979), which can also be transmitted trans-generationally as nameless places or dark secrets (see Kestenberg 1980). Their perpetuation follows the paths of unconscious phantasies (Isaacs 1948), frequently expressed 'beyond words' in moods, gestures or ominous silences. They penetrate into the psyche almost silently using elementary processes of communication such as projective and introjective identification (see Klein 1946; Frank & Weiss 2007; Spillius & O'Shaughnessy 2012).

Furthermore, the role of non-resonant, intrusive or violent relationships in the surroundings of early infancy has been highlighted, expressed either as an atmosphere of diffuse anxiety, overstimulation, lack of liveliness or dull despair. Leonard Shengold (1979) pointed out that it is often those negligent and cruel parents on whom the child depends in his despair that force him to resort to denial and splitting to preserve anything good. Coates & Moore (1997) further pointed out that in such cases later symbolic working through and transformation of the traumatic experiences are made even more difficult.

In contrast, André Green described a situation in his paper 'The dead mother' (Green 1983) in which the depressive mother, while physically present, remains internally absent so that she cannot be mourned. In this way, she is internalised as well as split off by the child leading to the psychic emptiness of a 'white depression'.

Peter Fonagy and colleagues (Fonagy 2001; Fonagy et al. 2002; Fonagy et al. 2003) have investigated the effect of early traumatic relationships on attachment behaviour and on the developing capacity for mentalisation. Such children tend to develop insecure and disorganised styles of relationships. They often react to conflict with panic and fear of death and have difficulties in distinguishing fantasy and reality. In stressful situations, their thinking remains concrete and they find it difficult 'to play with reality' (Fonagy & Target 2001). A consequence of this is that certain fixed behaviour patterns tend to become repetitive.

On the basis of Bion's (1962) developmental model, which emphasises the receiving and transforming function (*containment*) of the parental psyche in response to the primitive emotional experiences of the infant, Gianna Williams (1997) pointed out that when the primary relationship is a disturbed one, the relationship between *container* and *contained* may be reversed, so that the parents cannot absorb the emotional messages of their children but inversely project their own unbearable feelings into them. There, they trigger pathological identifications or remain as 'foreign bodies' in the infant's mind. Confusional states, processes of role reversal and feelings of guilt that are difficult to disentangle may be effects of this. Such elements can remain encapsulated for long periods of time or be hidden in healthier parts of the personality, so that they are not acknowledged but can suddenly unfurl their pathogenic effect in the context of external changes. Esther Horn described how a kind of 'fog' was spread within one of her female patients, which for a long time gave the illusion of gentleness, softness and unreality, while containing the nameless dread of fragmented, traumatic experiences of violence from her childhood (Horn & Weiss 2010).

A comprehensive account of the different developmental lines of psychoanalytic theories of trauma was provided by Werner Bohleber (2000). In a similar vein, Ira Brenner (2014) identifies the extensive links between individual, historic and societal trauma. With reference to the development of the individual, Franco De Masi (2015) described in a recent publication the emotional significance of early attachment relationships, the effect of different kinds of trauma and the subsequent protective and defensive manoeuvres as a complex interplay between external influences and internal processing mechanisms. Likewise, he emphasised the significance of processes of reparation in traumatised patients whose details and mechanisms, as he says, are not yet adequately understood (De Masi 2017).

The consequences of traumatic experiences

All these processes described by different authors have one thing in common: the damage leaves *permanent traces* or *silent zones of forgetting* in the psyche, variously described as a 'black hole' (Kinston & Cohen 1986) or an 'empty circle' (Laub 2000, p. 868). Many patients report sudden flashbacks, nightmares, primitive anxieties and confusional states. They lack the basic trust of a containing internal object and an active self, which could help them deal with the pressures of life (Bohleber 2010; 2017). They often feel unstable in their identity and are plagued by feelings of unreality and threat emanating from their environment, as well as from their own body. Bohleber (2017) names this as catastrophic loneliness, fear of death, hatred, shame and despair.

To protect against such feelings, splitting mechanisms are brought into play with the consequence that *areas of isolation* are created, either located in other places or in another time, only to burst out in the psyche at some other time as *dissociative states* (see Brenner 2001). They can affect single ego functions, such as the capacity to remember and perceive reality, but also subjective identity in states of depersonalisation (Bohleber 2017). Freud had already examined such splitting mechanisms in his exploration of fetishism (Freud 1927e) and later on in his paper 'Splitting of the ego in the process of defence' (Freud 1940e). They lead to a change in the ego's capacity to discriminate (see Freud 1925h) so that different and at times contradictory versions of reality can coexist, seemingly unquestioned.

Some patients resort to *pathological constructions* (De Masi 2015, p. 49) which appear to make the anxiety more bearable and seemingly bring order to the chaos. In this way, they provide a deceptive feeling of security, but actually impede psychic development and change. In the literature, such constructions have been described as '*bastions*' (Baranger & Baranger 2008), states of '*psychic retreat*' (Steiner 1993) or '*traumatic defence organisations*' (Brown 2005; 2006). What they have in common is that while they serve as a protective shield initially, in due course they become prisons that become difficult to escape from.

In these states, *agora- and claustrophobic anxieties* alter in quick succession. Henry Rey (1979) described this state where internal and external space enmesh as the 'agora-claustrophobic dilemma'. The patient either feels lost or stifled. The potential for relationships is limited and the internal experiences in the traumatic areas of their minds are often characterised by overwhelming *concreteness* (see Weiss 2015b).

The concreteness in turn is an expression of the difficulty to transform emotional experiences into symbols. Symbolisation presupposes the capacity to think presence in absence and to be able to bear absence in the presence. When this cannot be achieved, it results either in a *psychic vacuum* (see Riesenberg-Malcolm 2004) or in the occurrence of bizarre symptoms which are hardly distinguishable from sensory perception. Such *disturbances of symbol formation* are expressed in states of psychic emptiness, hypochondriacal anxieties or various other physical symptoms (Giovacchini 1993). They contain unconscious phantasies as well as unsymbolised fragments of memory. Parts of the body then become equated with menacing internal objects or form 'psychotic islands' (Rosenfeld 2001) in order to protect the self from further disintegration and splitting. Eating disorders, self-harm and attacks on one's own body are further prevalent symptoms, particularly in severe traumatisation.

A basic problem in dealing with these *embodied memories* (see Leu-zinger-Bohleber 2015) is that they correspond to 'unrepresented mental states' (see Levine et al. 2013) and have been cut off the rest of experience for a long time. They are expressed in characteristic difficulties to remember and to forget, so that the past can break immediately into the present or *a timeless zone of forgetting* develops.

Timelessness as a consequence of traumatic experiences has been discussed by various authors (Giovacchini 1967; Hartocollis 1978; 1983; Loewald 1980; Gutwinski-Jeggle 1992). Gerd Schmithüsen, who has summarised the literature on this topic, regards the 'freezing' of time as a desperate attempt 'to not be confronted with the anxiety of another breakdown' (Schmithüsen 2004, p. 295). However, it is exactly that which leaves the trauma encapsulated, cut off from the rest of experience and thus everlasting. Instead of 'time lived' (Bergson 1907) there is a 'dead space', which constantly denudes life of significance and meaning.

This similarly applies to states of *internal emptiness*, which are experienced as agonising by many patients resulting in the seeking of distraction in the form of stimulants, sexual excitement, promiscuity, self-harm or intoxicating activities. Not uncommonly, an addictive dependency on such activities develops (see Joseph 1982). For a short period of time, they let the patient forget the despair, but lead to a strengthening of the feeling of hopelessness in the long run.

The *pressure to act* is not just in relation to getting rid of thoughts by doing something, but also extends into interpersonal relationships. When it is impossible to think about feelings, primitive, basic means are deployed to expel the unbearable and transmit it into others. In this way, the patients put pressure on people they are close to, burden them with feelings and enmesh them in scenarios which actualise unconscious phantasies. In therapy, the perpetrator–victim relationship is frequently re-enacted either openly or in more subtle ways, particularly as 'the patient...may not able...to tolerate the therapist's concerned but neutral position, which runs counter to the overriding need to divide the world into allies and enemies' (Kernberg 2008, p. 42). In order to register and understand these re-enactments, the working through of the counter-transference assumes central significance in the analytic situation (see Joseph 1971; 1985; 1989; Jacobs 1986; 1993; McLaughlin 1987; 1991; Gabbard 1995).

Lawrence Brown (2005, p. 398) has described the *charging of the analyst with counter-transference feelings*, the repetitive recurrence of enmeshed relationships and the impairment of symbolic thinking as typical elements of a rigid traumatic defence organisation. Referring back to Bion (1962) he uses the term of a '*β-screen*', which serves to expel indigestible elements (β-elements) that cannot be translated into 'dream thoughts' by the psyche. Clinically this is expressed by patients as 'feeling as if in a foreign body', as well as in a tendency to produce dreams which seem to be desperate attempts to rid the self of traumatic affect rather than being expressions of internal images.

Ultimately, many traumatised patients are in the grip of a *cruel super-ego*. Shame and guilt feelings then assume a persecutory quality, paralyse psychic function and damage the relationship with good internal objects (Brenman 2006). Instead of enabling mourning, repetitive cycles are being established which perpetuate the damage, severely impede or even prevent reparative processes. In order for these processes to unfold, the super-ego has to develop into a less cruel, more receptive and forgiving structure. Conversely, however, such an evolution of the super-ego depends on the transformation of relatively primitive reparative manoeuvres to mature processes of reparation.

Reparation, repetition compulsion and guilt – a psychoanalytic paradigm

This transformation of the super-ego will be the focus of the following deliberations. What is the difference between mature and pathological reparation? What developmental steps does it take to overcome abasement, humiliation and persecutory guilt? How does resentment, shame and rage block the path to reparation? What exactly is the connection between the failure of reparation and the repetition compulsion? What are the pre-conditions which gradually enable the patient to slowly relinquish the protection of their pathological organisation? What role do memory and forgetting play to re-integrate parts of the biography which have fallen out of history and to regain the relationship with subjective time? What does forgiveness mean in such a context? And how can envy and resentment be overcome in order to develop a capacity for gratitude?

All these questions make the path of reparation appear a difficult one posing many dangers on its way. It can fall by the wayside, get stuck in dead ends or get lost in labyrinths. Nevertheless, it is often the unconscious wish for reparation which prompts the patient to seek treatment. According to Henry Rey (1986; 1988) it is therefore as important to seek out these hidden efforts at reparation as it is to investigate the obstacles which obstruct its way. For it is only when compassion, sorrow and forgiveness gradually emerge that stuck situations can, at least partially, be reversed (Rey 1994, p. 204).

The concept of 'reparation' occurs relatively late in psychoanalytic literature. In her analyses of children, Melanie Klein (1932) met situations in which her young patients expressed deep sorrow about the damaged state of their play figures and phantasy objects (see Frank 2009). This can be exemplified by a drawing of the six-year-old obsessive-compulsive Erna (Figure 1), which shows the mother in heaven while the 'bad girl' who pulled down her pants and smashed her benches and chairs is burning in hell. The mother is surrounded by three devils, one laughing ('Ein lachender Teufel'), one crying ('Ein weinender Teufel') and a third one, close to 'St Peter in the clouds' is comforting her ('Ein Teufel, der die Mutter tröstet', see Weiss & Frank 1996, p. 131).

In a recent paper, Claudia Frank (2012) has vividly depicted the transitions from phantasised destruction, alarm and reparation by means of the drawings and play sequences of Klein's patients. These moments were accompanied by intense feelings of sadness and guilt,

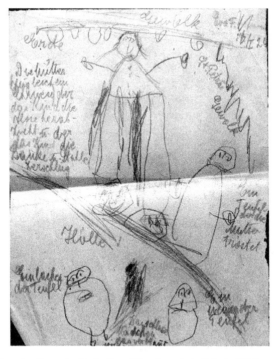

Figure 1 Drawing from the beginning of Erna's analysis (16. 1. 1924)
Reproduced with permission from the Melanie Klein Trust, London.

together with the endeavour to put things back together, to preserve them and give them a place internally. In due course, Klein assigned these actions to the 'depressive position' (Klein 1946) where splitting can be overcome and projections can be taken back.

It is only when splitting can be overcome that 'good' and 'bad' parts can be linked together and can be perceived in the self as well as in the other. The emerging feeling of *separateness* becomes pivotal for all further development: for the development of *processes of symbolisation* (Segal 1957; 1978; 1991); for the unfolding of an *internal space* as distinguished from a separate external space (Rey 1979; 1994); for the development of a *sense of time* (Colarusso 1979; Arlow 1984; 1986; Bell 2006); and for the experience of the *continuity of the life history,* as well as for the establishment of genuine interpersonal relationships, in which the other person is not just a reflection of one's own internal objects.

Where reparation fails or gets stuck these developments are blocked. As early as 1936, Joan Rivière described a state in which the individual can neither repair their internal objects nor escape them: a dilemma in which she saw a possible reason for therapeutic failure.

Beyond the boundaries of psychology, the concept of reparation is of universal significance in cultural and humanitarian history (see Potter 2015). Likewise processes of regeneration and reparation play a central part in all *biological processes.* They are crucial in overcoming damage and in facilitating new life. The programmed death of cells, apoptosis, is a mechanism which protects the organism by preventing their unhindered proliferation (see Potten & Wilson 2004). The body's own operant antibiotic peptides, the so-called defensins, are subject to a complex auto-regulation with the aim of maintaining the integrity of the mucous barrier in order to avoid an immune reaction directed against the body's own tissue (Wehkamp & Stange 2015, p. 27).

Reparative enzymes are assigned the task of identifying damages in the genetic make-up and to replace mutated DNA sequences with the right base sequences and nucleotides (Lindahl & West 1995). In this way, spontaneous mutations and damages through external influences cannot affect the cell cycle and the cell metabolism in an unlimited way.

Correspondingly, one could hypothesise that in psychic processes *it is not so much the particular traumatic experiences which lead to long term damage, but those experiences which interfere with the natural integrity of the processes of reparation.* Such a view has ramifications for treatment in that its task is not only seen as reconstructing particular experiences, but to regain a *capacity for reparation.* This might imply a possible contribution to the psychoanalytic study of resilience (see Southwick & Charney

2012) as was shown in research investigating the fate of children who survived the Holocaust (Ornstein 1981; 1985; Krystal 2000; Held 2014).

There are numerous parallels in societal, social and cultural contexts beyond the individual. What does reconciliation mean in the face of murder, persecution and displacement which will never be redressed? Can we address reparation at all in a context of a breakdown of civilisation, as in the Holocaust? How are mutual understanding and fairness possible in view of the unequal distribution of power? Why does splitting into friend and enemy promote the transition from disappointment and difference into hostility and violence (Schöpf 2005, p. 165)? Why is the 'barrier of guilt' skipped over in these conditions so that sorrow becomes impossible but instead a cycle of revenge is set going 'handing on the unresolved problem to the next generations and into history' (ibid.)? How does it come that the vulnerability of the other, which the philosopher Emmanuel Lévinas (1978) dealt with in great detail in his late work[3], cannot be seen any longer?

Is there something like a repetition compulsion in history when guilt is blended out and traumatic experiences cannot be worked through? Finally, is it at all possible to have a rapprochement with terror without setting it off again or being engulfed by it? How can the unfolding of destructiveness be limited and how can the breaks caused by traumatic experiences be fitted back into a continuity of history? Werner Bohleber (2010) pursued these connections in his book *Destructiveness, Intersubjectivity and Trauma*. In particular, he emphasised the necessity of regaining historic remembering. Here, I can only refer to his comprehensive account of the various psychoanalytic approaches on this topic.

Madeleine and Willy Baranger in co-operation with Jorge Mario Mom (1988, p. 116) argued in a similar way that the concept described by Freud as *Nachträglichkeit* ('afterwardness') implies the possibility of re-introducing traumatic experiences back into history at a later stage and to regain them in an altered form. Just as the here and now in the transference is always interwoven with the past and the future (see Riesenberg-Malcolm 1986; Weiss 1988). It is in this way, that Dana Birksted-Breen interprets Winnicott's statement (1964) that the 'breakdown' which the patient unconsciously dreads has already happened, as an expression of the fact that the analytic treatment provides a setting in which the circumstance of the traumatic experiences can be re-lived and symbolised (Birksted-Breen 2003, p. 1513).

A fundamental question in this is the problem of *regaining history and remembrance*. This task was broached very early on by phenomenological psychiatrists such as Erwin Straus (1930) in whose view it was only possible to 'extract meaning' from the trauma if what has occurred can be re-translated into the dimension of *subjective experience*. The French philosopher Paul Ricoeur (1998; 2004) has described processes of *historisation*, which come into play in the reconstruction of history and which he characterised as 'containing forgetting' and 'heavy forgiveness'. I will come back to this at a later stage.

Looking at this in the wider context, the question of how feelings of guilt are dealt with in relation to processes of reparation assumes a central position. To put it simply, without the experience of guilt there is no reason for reparation. In relation to treatment technique, Klein has always insisted on this connection.[4]

But what are the pre-conditions that make it possible to experience guilt? And how is guilt made up, how heavy must it weight to enable reparation?

Melanie Klein has described the transition from the paranoid-schizoid to the depressive position as largely a transition from *persecutory* to *depressive guilt*. Distressed, depressive guilt can be preserved and held in the individual, whereas persecutory guilt has to be expelled and relocated in another. It is then these others by whom one feels persecuted and whose fault it is that one is doomed.

Accordingly, the experience of *depressive guilt* presupposes a certain integration of love and hate feelings towards the person one feels dependent upon. Only where love and hate come together in relation to the *same* object can feelings of guilt develop. As long as these feelings are kept apart and distributed onto different persons there is no reason for experiencing guilt. Because there is no need for reparation towards an infinitely good, idealised figure, just as there is no need for feelings of guilt towards an exclusively bad figure. This is exactly what Klein (1946; 1957) meant by the concept of *splitting* (see also Spillius et al. 2011, p. 491, Blass 2015; Weiss 2015a).

Splitting in its simplest, most elementary form leads to a separation of 'good' parts of the self, linked in with idealised internal figures from 'bad' parts of the self, which in turn are tied in with evil, persecutory objects. In a world which is dominated by splitting there is only black and white, good or bad, friend or foe. It is only when the splitting mechanisms abate that the individual discovers that it is the *same counterpart* whom they love and hate, who disappoints them as well as provides gratification. And it is only now that there is a space for the development of sorrow, empathy and guilt.

However, feelings of guilt need a place where they can be contained and thus be made more bearable. Above all, they need *time* to be worked through. Freud (1923b) described this space–time structure as the *super-ego* and linked it to the internalised parental figures. But this super-ego also contains parts of the primitive self and is not a constant but an oscillating structure, cruel and persecutory in its archaic form, but boundary setting and supportive in its more mature state.

Depending on how the super-ego relates to the developing self, it can either support or hinder the development of the self. On the one hand, under the dominance of an 'ego destroying super-ego' (Bion 1962, p. 98) feelings of guilt can assume a persecutory quality and threaten the developing self. On the other hand, under a more benign super-ego, processes of reparation can be initiated. Melanie Klein has described this evolution of the super-ego in detail in her essay 'On the development of mental functioning' (Klein 1958). In a similar vein, Nunberg (1926) distinguished between a sense of guilt as an expression of the life instinct and the need for punishment as an expression of the death instinct. Hans Loewald's (1962a, b; 1980) explorations into the relationship of the super-ego and the development of the sense of time go in the same direction. He hypothesises that the developing, mature super-ego makes 'psychological time' accessible and thus enables forward-looking development, expectation, creativity and hope.

Creativity implies overcoming stagnation and a sense of opening oneself to the passage of time. Only when loss can be mourned can a space for creative development evolve. This applies to the life of the individual no less than to the work of the artist. The relationship between reparation and artistic creativity has been highlighted in particular by Hanna Segal in her deliberations on aesthetics (Segal 1952; 1981; 1991). She distinguishes *genuine reparation* from *manic* and *omnipotent forms* of reparation. The former presupposes a 'renunciation of omnipotence and magic', the emergence of guilt and the 'acceptance (...) of psychic reality'.

> The acceptance of psychic reality involves the renunciation of omnipotence and magic, the lessening of splitting and the withdrawal of projective identification. It means the acceptance of the idea of separateness- the differentiation of one's own self from one's parents with all the conflict this implies. It also involves, as part of reparation, allowing one's object to be free, to love and restore one another without depending on oneself.
>
> (Segal, 1964, p. 102)

So our first approach is that the need for reparation only develops when feelings of guilt (G) can be experienced. This is based on the premise that there has been a connection between love (L) and hate (H) towards the same object (O) for some time in which both feelings overlap.

(1) $L \cap H \rightarrow O = G$

This connection is initially often short lived and unstable. Under pressure from primitive anxiety it can collapse very easily so that processes of splitting are deployed once more. In order to give it more durability and stability, a holding structure, namely the super-ego (SE), is needed to transform the emerging guilt feelings into a bearable shape. The developing integration leads to the emergence of processes of reparation (R), which in turn facilitate further mental development.

(2) $G \cap SE \rightarrow R$

In her already mentioned work from 1958, Klein emphasises that in this case the super-ego takes on the function of the mother, who contains and modifies the primitive anxieties of her infant, encourages and comforts him or her, but, at the same time, sets boundaries:

> The super-ego – being bound up with the good object and even striving for its preservation – comes close to the actual good mother who feeds the child and takes care of it, but since the super-ego is also under the influence of the death instinct, it partly becomes the representative of the mother who frustrates the child, and its prohibitions and accusations arouse anxiety. To some extent, when development goes well, the super-ego is largely felt as helpful and does not operate as too harsh a conscience.
>
> (Klein 1958, p. 240)

Klein had already described in an earlier paper that the mother *contains* the projected 'bad' parts of the self (Klein 1946, p. 8). In this sense, maternal love for and understanding are 'the infant's greatest stand-by in overcoming states of disintegration and anxieties of a psychotic nature' (ibid. p. 10). Bion (1962) has named this process *containment* and linked it with maternal *reverie*.

With the attenuation of persecutory anxiety, the super-ego gradually develops into an entity which facilitates integration, reparation and reality orientation. The injured object is now 'no longer predominantly felt as a persecutor, but as a loved object towards whom a feeling of guilt and the urge to make reparation are experienced' (Klein 1958, p. 242). However, this is not a permanent accomplishment. Klein rather thought that the archaic, 'terrifying figures' exist life-long and can make themselves felt in the deep layers of the unconscious under 'extreme internal and external pressure' even under 'favourable circumstances' (ibid. p. 243). Such 'pressures' may be equivalent to those emanating from a traumatic situation.

Loewald (1962a) too linked the development of the super-ego closely with 'experiences of separation, of loss and restitution' which are 'in many ways similar to mourning' (p. 484). His analysis of the relationship between mourning, reparation and internalisation is in many ways close to Klein's although in a different theoretical framework (see Loewald 1980).

Super-ego and reparation are thus in a complex interrelationship. On the one hand, the capacity for reparation is dependent on the availability of a relatively benign super-ego. On the other hand, such a super-ego can only develop when projections are taken back and processes of reparation are activated. This is a problem which not only Klein encountered in her early child analyses (see Steiner 2017), but James Strachey (1934) touched on it in his paper on the 'mutative transference interpretation'.

(3) SE ↔ R

It becomes clear from this somewhat schematic overview that processes of reparation are vulnerable and fragile. They can fail on the level of integration of love and hate, because the resulting connection is experienced as too threatening. On the other hand, the predominance of an archaic super-ego does not allow a genuine integration and processing of feelings of guilt, so that they are either experienced as persecutory or directed against the own self.

Feelings of resentment, anger or shame can obstruct attempts at reparation because the need for revenge, the entitlement of moral superiority or the tendency to withdraw often emanate from them. The wish for reparation then gets stuck somewhere along the way, so to speak, and ends up in a dead end obstructing the unfolding of relationships that promote development.

Ultimately, under the influence of primitive defensive processes *omnipotent and concrete forms of thinking* prevail so that 'reparation' only seems possible in the form of undoing or as a concrete re-creation through action. Following general English linguistic use, Ursula Ostendorf (2012) has distinguished these forms of reparation as *repair* from mature forms of *reparation*. Examples of primitive reparation are the *manic reparation* (Klein 1935; Winnicott 1935) of certain narcissistic and borderline patients or the *compulsive reparation*, where omnipotent, magical and sadistic tendencies are mixed in with efforts of reparation (Klein 1935).

Interestingly, such *processes of restitution* were described by other authors at the time Klein introduced the concept of 'reparation' into the psychoanalytic literature. Initially, Klein used the term synonymously with 'restoration' (see Spillius et al. 2011) and only later systematically explored reparation, the overcoming of splitting and the beginning of the depressive position when contradictory emotions are linked and integrated into the self. Herman Nunberg (1931 [1929]) spoke in a similar way of the 'the synthetic capacity of the ego (…) [which] manifests itself (…) as follows: it assimilates alien elements (both from within and from without), and it mediates between opposing elements and even reconciles opposites and sets mental productivity in train.' (pp. 121–122). In this way, the damage done to the loved objects in phantasy can be overcome and reparation becomes a 'fundamental element of love and all human relationships' (Klein 1937, p. 313).

These developments linking the experience of guilt and the renunciation of omnipotence are distinguished from the *substitute constructions* of psychotic patients, although they too are aimed at the removal of damage. As early as 1920, Nunberg described the delusional restitution fantasy of 're-birth' in a case of a catatonic schizophrenic patient who tried to avert his fear of the 'end of the world'. The best-known example of such a psychotic restitution is Freud's (1911c) case of the analysis of the notes of the paranoid president of the senate, Daniel Paul Schreber, whose complex delusional system he regarded as an attempt to compensate for the psychotic experience of the end of the world through creating a re-constructive substitution.

'The delusional formation, which we take to be the pathological product, is in reality an attempt at recovery, a process of reconstruction' (ibid. p. 70). In 1924, he adds that 'the delusion is found applied like a patch over the place *where originally a rent had appeared in the ego's relation to the external world.*' (Freud 1924b, p. 150; italics mine).

Schreber was in many ways, as we know today, a traumatised patient and his notes which were published under the title 'Memoirs of my Nervous Illness' (Schreber 1903) can be understood as an attempt to deal with his traumatic childhood experiences as well as with his later psychotic breakdown (see Katan 1959; Niederland 1959a, b; Lothane 1992; Steiner 2004).

Reparation and symbol formation

However, there is a world of difference between these powerful, psychotic attempts at restitution, which are like a glued joint trying to connect the torn relationship to reality, the magic attempts at reparation, which one finds in neurotic, narcissistic and borderline patients and those efforts at reparation which acknowledge mourning and loss thus facilitating an approach to reality through creative symbol formation. The latter form the basis of artistic work.

Hanna Segal was the one disciple of Melanie Klein who explored the connection between reparation and artistic creativity in depth following on from Klein's early work on symbol formation (Klein 1930). The artist has the need, as she put it, to 're-create what he feels in the depth of his internal world' (Segal 1991 p. 86). This work has no conclusion and is never finished. 'The act of creation at depth has to do with an unconscious memory of an harmonious internal world and the experience of its destruction; that is the depressive position. The impulse is to recover and recreate this lost world.' (ibid. p. 94)

The paradoxical situation that the work of the artist is new but at the same time arises from the need to re-construct is part of the nature of symbol formation in as much as creative imagination touches on the pain and despair of loss. In this way, dreams, artistic creativity and play are different from reproductive daydreams, which do not explore external or internal reality, but are often 'as-if worlds' (Deutsch 1934; Riesenberg-Malcolm 1990). Segal elaborates:

> The symbol is not a copy of the object- it is something created anew. The world the artist creates is created anew. This too has to do with a reparative reconstruction. It is a restoring in one's internal world of a parental couple creating a new baby.
>
> (Segal 1991, p. 95)

Successful reparation, whether in the therapeutic work, in interpersonal relationships or in artistic creation, is thus linked to processes of symbol formation.

In the following chapters, different forms of successful and failed reparation will be investigated in patients who were exposed to severe and chronic traumatisation during their childhoods. One of the theses represented here claims that failing reparation leads into the vicious circle of the *repetition compulsion*. Instead of contributing to reparation, the repetition compulsion perpetuates the damage to the internal objects, which in turn further reinforces the experience of powerlessness, paralysis and crushing guilt. At the same time, the repetition compulsion brings about a state of *timelessness* in which there is a continuing recurrence of the same.

Many authors have described the relationship of traumatic experiences and the repetition compulsion (see Bohleber 2000; 2007; Laub & Lee 2003; Brenner 2014) and linked it, particularly Laub (2000), with Freud's (1920g) hypothesis of the death instinct as the destructive powers take on a momentum of their own. The enmeshment of trauma and repetition becomes all the more rigid the more concrete and primitive forms of thinking predominate instead of more mature, symbolic thought processes, because it is only the capacity of forming symbols for emotional experiences that opens a space for recognition and understanding (Henningsen 2000; 2008; 2012).

But long before the child can use symbolic forms of communication, the experience of being understood is conveyed through the gaze in his earliest relationships. This gaze can express love, affection and affirmation, but also anxiety, horror, reproach or rejection. It becomes the basis of self-esteem and all further relationships. As Claudia Frank (2015a) has shown in a recent paper, the gaze can lose its exploratory, reciprocal and receptive function under the influence of a cruel super-ego and assume an intrusive, condemnatory and even destructive quality.

In order to avoid experiences of humiliation and shame, narcissistic organisations are frequently brought into play to lend an apparent feeling of strength and moral superiority. The reproach is then no longer directed against the self but against others. Such distortions of the gaze can lead to long term enmeshments which impede mutual understanding and in therapy take effect as a resistance to psychic change.

Preview of further chapters

The function of the gaze in states of resentment, shame and wrath will be examined in Chapter 2 of this book. In contrast to other early sensory modalities such as taste, smell, touch and hearing, seeing introduces *distance* between the self and the other, which not only conveys a first sense of separation, but also a reciprocal experience of *being seen* (Steiner 2011a). The experience of seeing and being seen can, however, take on very different forms. While the gaze is directed accusingly from below to above in resentment, the ashamed person faces an object that looks down on him or her with a demeaning look. In contrast, in rage and wrath the gaze is directed from above to below in a condemnatory way.

All of these feelings can become the source of pathological organisations manifesting themselves as *states of psychic retreat* (see Steiner 1993). Because of their complex structure, they tend to involve others in their function which contributes to their rigidity and resistance to change. Clinical vignettes will be used to describe the transition from resentment to shame and wrath. In doing so, the direction of gaze can be reversed and the eye will then be used to invade and control the object (see Steiner 2006a), just as resentment and shame, rage and wrath can be used to circumvent feelings of sadness and guilt. In this way, efforts of reparation are blocked, transforming these feelings into chronic states of mind and thereby posing considerable technical challenges. While the themes of justice and hurt play an important role in resentment and shame, the basis of wrath seems to be a fundamentalist conviction of a moral or religious kind. The latter is not only seen in individual pathologies, but is also reflected in group phenomena and societal processes.

In Chapter 3, the highly organised forms of resentment and rage are retraced in the example of a borderline patient. The case history will exemplify the patient's pursuit of power and control based on his childhood background of being hurt and humiliated. When his defence system collapsed because of external circumstances, he withdrew into a self-destructive state of moaning and angry contempt, in which reparation was only possible if others were to admit to their mistakes, to undo what was done and to compensate him for the injustice he had suffered – all of this without any possibility of reconciliation. The enormous destructiveness emanating from this position manifested itself in suicidal threats as well as in an attitude of moral superiority which initially made him experience the analytic treatment as renewed humiliation.

In the course of therapy, the same constellations of relationships which formed the basis of his pathological construct, gradually re-emerged. In particular, it was the demands for reparation which were transferred to the analyst with the result that he was exposed to the same experiences of failure and guilt as the patient had been under the unbearable dominance of his archaic super-ego. In several treatment vignettes, I will try to show that the analyst ran the risk of re-projecting the feelings received from the patient in an equally reproachful way back into him. Only when this dilemma was acknowledged and gradually worked through were there moments when the omnipotent illusion of undoing could be overcome, guilt could become more bearable and genuine reparation became possible in small steps.

Some patients who were exposed to the experience of overwhelming violence in early life respond to their trauma by constructing highly complex phantasy structures which almost reverse those traumatic experiences into their opposite. The structure and function of such a defensive organisation will be explored in Chapter 4 using the case of a severely traumatised female patient suffering from chronic depression, problems of identity and a tendency to self-harm. In her daydreams, which often served as an aid in going to sleep, she retreated into the imaginary sanctuary of a 'tower', in which the torturers and tormentors of her childhood became her 'best friends'. There she seemed protected from her persecutory anxieties, as long as she submitted herself to the demands of her tormentors without complaint. The illusory feeling of security which the 'men in the tower' provided enabled her to survive under difficult conditions, but made her feel any wish for development or change to be a betrayal.

Using clinical material from the course of treatment, a detailed examination of the developing relation between the defensive organisation and the transference situation will be presented. Initially, the analyst was perceived as a powerful figure, who offered the patient security at the price of submission and control. In a second phase, a conflict of loyalty evolved where she felt torn between the analysis and her cruel internal figures. Following this, the existing splitting broke down and in a temporary state of chaos and confusion the long-standing protective mechanisms of discipline and submission proofed to be no longer useful. In a further vignette, a re-integration could be observed in which the now weakened defence organisation co-existed alongside with the new developments allowing the patient new, although limited freedoms in her life.

In Chapter 5, the possibilities and limitations of reparation in severely traumatised patients will be investigated with further clinical material. With detailed vignettes from the same patient, I will argue that the disturbing experiences have to be lived through in the transference and counter-transference in order to regain lost parts of the self and to initiate a process of mourning. 'Reparation' here means more than mere forgiveness, but refers to an inner process of reconstruction, overcoming as well as acknowledging the damages of the past. This form of reparation refers primarily to the unconscious identification with the destructive object, to the development of a less cruel super-ego as well as to the frequently painful regaining of lost parts of the self.

In this process, the possibility of remembering plays as important a role as the possibility of forgetting. Both are linked to the analyst's capacity to absorb and work with the damaged objects in a way that neither overwhelms him nor makes him push them back into the patient, finding them unbearable. This encompasses enactments the analyst will be more or less unavoidably drawn into, the regaining of psychic space and of symbolic thinking as a pre-condition of the acknowledgement of the patient's history, but also a realistic evaluation of the possibilities and limitations of the analytic process.

The literary work of Jenny Erpenbeck exemplifies that traumatic experiences do not only cause ruptures in individuals but also in collective history and in a tragic way therefore lead to repetition. This dual structure of a torn, but continuously recurring, history forms the central point of her deliberations on the riddle of time scattered throughout her work. In Chapter 6, her novel *The End of Days* will be the starting point for thinking about the role of remembering and forgetting in view of traumatic experiences, as for instance Nanette Auerhahn and Dori Laub have done in their work on the difficulties of remembering after severe psychological trauma (Auerhahn & Laub 1984; Laub & Auerhahn 1993).

Traumatic remembering has the effect that the past is always present, always recurring, never past, while *ecliptic forgetting* affects a kind of obliteration, which leaves an empty space in the self by erasing the traces of the past. In contrast, the concepts of *containing forgetting* and *forgiving remembering* (Ricoeur 1998) are about reinstating the continuity of history.

A theory of remembering, which takes up these differences, touches on the psychological significance of mourning and guilt. It is only when the individual can face these emotional experiences that reparation in its mature form can take place. Therefore the relationship between *reparation* and *gratitude* will be explored in Chapter 7. Different forms of genuine and pathological gratitude will be illustrated with different clinical cases. Reparation depends on a primary capacity for gratitude in the sense of overcoming envy. At the same time, the development of gratitude can only emerge after processes of reparation have begun. This paradox comes to the fore in the final phase of analysis when analyst and patient have to come to the often-painful acknowledgement of the passing of time and the limits of all good experiences. But, to use one of Hanna Segal's thoughts, it is only because these good experiences are finite, that the bad experiences cannot go on forever either.

Notes

1 Jean Laplanche (1987) comprehensively returns to Freud's starting point when he describes in his 'general seduction theory' the irreducible asymmetry between the 'enigmatic messages' of the adults and immature psyche of the child as the 'basic anthropological situation', which 'no human being can avoid' (Laplanche 2004, p. 899). These messages are like a 'foreign body in the psyche' (ibid. p. 902) which can only retrospectively be integrated, registered and translated when the necessary capacities have evolved. If these are missing, the development of psychotic structures is promoted.

2 Letter to Wilhelm Fließ from 21st September 1897.

3 Lévinas (1978) emphasises passivity and guilt in the situation the ego is placed in. 'The persecution brings the ego back to itself, to the absolute accusative in which there is imputed to the ego a fault it has not committed or willed, and which confounds it in its freedom. Egoism and altruism are posterior to responsibility (…). Persecution is a trauma, violence par excellence (…) [it] leads back to a resignation not consented to, and consequently crosses a night of unconsciousness. That is the sense of the unconscious, night in which the reverting of the ego into itself under the trauma of persecution occurs, a passivity more passive still than every passivity on this side of identity, responsibility, substitution' (p. 197).

4 See recently published lectures on technique by Klein (1936) as well as Steiner's (2017) extensive introductory comments.

Chapter 2

Impediments to reparation

Resentment, shame and wrath – the significance of the gaze

Among the feelings arising from harm and trauma, which can often be traced back to childhood, we frequently find resentment, shame and rage/wrath in our patients. From their descriptions, we gather that these are not simply affective states, but highly organised internal stances which are more or less embedded in all their interpersonal relationships. Closer inspection reveals that these feelings are closely connected with wide-ranging fantasies. There seems to be a particular sensitivity towards unfairness, being shamed or insulted. These feelings emerge very rapidly during treatment and we frequently have the experience that resentment, shame and rage are extraordinarily difficult to change; despite being able to trace their history and origin and to understand their significance in the present, they nevertheless have a tendency to perpetuate themselves. Then, what we say to the patient will be experienced as a renewed insult and in turn will serve as a justification to maintain the very state we actually set out to change. One gets the impression that these emotional stances are something highly complex in which the analyst gets easily drawn into and entangled. They have a tendency to maintain the status quo, even though this might be linked with pain and suffering for the patient.

A phenomenological approach suggests that the gaze plays an essential part in all three feelings. In grievance, the gaze is directed *from below to above* in an accusatory, reproachful way, usually towards a powerful object, by whom one feels treated unfairly. In contrast, in humiliation and shame, being seen by the other implies a being *looked down on* sneeringly. On the contrary, in rage and wrath, we look *down on the other from above* in a contemptuous way, from a superior, self-righteous position.

What these emotional states have in common is that they are closely linked to the experience of *seeing and being seen.* The more pathological the underlying personality constellation, the more accusatory, demeaning or scathing the experience of the gaze. Although there are considerable

differences between shame, resentment and rage, there is a further simi-
larity in that they pose massive obstacles to the therapeutic task of working through mourning and guilt. In one way or another, they all imply a
self-righteous attitude, which feeds the need to retreat or take revenge.
This stands in the way of processes of reparation, which could provide the
chance of reconciliation and mutual understanding.

Therapeutically, we are therefore faced with the question of how to
change these stances without getting drawn too much into them. It is
difficult to interpret resentment without giving renewed cause for hurt
and offence. On occasion, it seems almost impossible to interpret humiliation without exposing the patient to a renewed experience of it. It can
prove to be a very tetchy matter to take up rage without provoking anger
and contempt. The tendency of these states to stabilise themselves, and to
immunise themselves against change, poses a considerable technical
challenge. It can prompt therapists to either enter into confrontation with
the patient or else to resign and to retreat. I will go on to show that both
ways of reacting will lead into typical impasses in therapy.

Resentment

Resentment has its origins in a feeling of having been treated *unfairly or
unjustly,* and cries out for settlement and compensation. Heinrich von
Kleist's (1810) *Michael Kohlhaas* is a classic example of this. This heigh-
tened sensitivity towards unfairness is generally related to early experiences of being left out and disappointed. While in the beginning there is
often a wish for compensation, in due course a tendency to hold on to the
grievances develops. The feeling of being aggrieved is now protected as if
it were a precious possession one must not let go of and which in turn
becomes a source of gratification through suffering. The resulting paradox is that the demand for compensation is never really allowed to reach
a genuine reconciliation. Instead, the wounds are kept open to nourish the
wishes for revenge and retaliation emanating from them. In this way,
grievance serves to maintain 'a bitter resentful feeling of deprivation'
(Feldman 2008), because the belief is that it is entirely the other's obligation to eliminate injustice, pain and envy. From a phenomenological
viewpoint, it was Max Scheler (1915), who emphasised the suppressed
enmity underlying resentment as a central characteristic of 'grievance', a
phenomenon he referred to as 'self-poisoning of the soul'.

The complaint of the aggrieved is frequently directed at a figure by
whom he felt deceived by withholding longed-for love and attention. At
other times, it refers to a feeling that a given promise has not been kept or
a prospect that was offered did not come to fruition. Frequently, the

person in question had been idealised before and the endeavour of the aggrieved is to re-establish the idealised relationship, which is one reason why compensation and reparation are not really thought possible. In grievance, the gaze is directed in a reproachful way *from below to above,* whereby the other is blamed for all the cruelty that has been inflicted.

The voracity of resentment, the gnawing feeling that emanates from it and the way it poisons thinking, indicate the oral origins of the disappointments on which it is based. In this way the reproachful gaze allows rage and guilt to be put into the other. The German word 'Vorwurf' (throwing at) is a literal translation of 'projection'. The 'vorwurfsvolle' (reproachful) gaze is directed from below to above. It does not serve as a recognition of reality, but as a way to apportion blame onto someone else. It is this mighty 'Other' that emits injustice and cruelty, and one's own wishes for retaliation and revenge are only intended to re-establish a state of 'fairness'. What remains unacknowledged, however, is that these wishes go far beyond the original aim, that they develop a life of their own and do not let the subject off the hook, but plague and torture him, just as the 'Other' is not given a chance to redeem himself by being benign or accommodating the aggrieved. In the extreme, when resentment is based on 'near delusional beliefs' (Feldman 2008), any such attempt at appeasement will be seen as a renewed deceit or else as an admission of guilt, which gives rise to new accusations and criticisms.

At times, one can observe that the original idealised state persists alongside the grievance and indignation. The analyst is then offered the opportunity to join in the splitting: either side with the patient and support them in their campaign against those objects who treated them unfairly in their childhood and continue to hurt and demean them, or become one of those unfair people, who instead of offering help, blames the patient for their difficulties.

There are many considerable challenges for treatment technique in this, which Melanie Klein already referred to in 1936 in the sixth of her lectures on treatment technique, where she says:

> It is not easy to find one's way between lack of sympathy on the one hand and the other extreme of colluding with the patient. I see a technical problem here, that is, perhaps more than many other technical problems, intimately bound up with the attitude of the analyst and his frame of mind.
>
> (Steiner 2017, p. 80)

Klein is adamant in her insistence that these reproachful and hostile impulses have to be taken up and examined in the transference. Frequently, such impulses emerge when the analyst does not fulfil the intended role of fellow accuser and 'ally'. Unnoticed, he/she is then implicated in the role of the unfair and hurtful figure. A short clinical vignette will illustrate this.

Clinical vignette

Mr. A., a restaurant owner in his mid-forties, had originally come from a southern European country where his father worked as a gamekeeper on a large ducal estate. With considerable hard work, he had established an independent livelihood in Germany; an effort, he felt, that was never sufficiently appreciated by his ageing parents who preferred his brother, who lived near them. Mr. A. had two children with his good-looking German wife, for whom he was envied by everybody. His misfortune began when he found out that his wife had betrayed him for years with another man. They separated and eventually divorced. In the course of this, the wife achieved a beneficial financial settlement and got both children to side with her. In his attempt to re-establish justice, Mr. A. consulted numerous lawyers and financial advisers, permanently feeling inadequately supported, exploited and finally swindled out of his right by the German justice system's discrimination against him as a foreigner.

When, during this period, a regular patron complained about a special game dish prepared by him, he fell ill with chronic depression accompanied by numerous psychosomatic complaints. He could no longer work in his restaurant. Controls by the public health department and the trade inspectorate reinforced his conviction that he had fallen victim to harassment. Eventually, he got someone else to do his work, and hid in his flat throughout the day, only visiting the restaurant secretly early in the morning or late at night, in order to check administrative matters or to procure supplies.

The initial assessment interview with Mr. A. was filled with endless accusations and protestations about his hitherto unsuccessful treatments. He spoke full of contempt about his father's subservience, who bowed very low, nearly touching the floor, when the duke came to visit the estate. He demonstrated this movement to me and looked at me full of humility.

When I put it to him that he approached me in a very similar way as his father approached the duke, his gaze shifted to one of hurt and accusation. Full of resentment, he conveyed the feeling of not being taken seriously or even being mocked by me. Very quickly I became identified with those divorce lawyers, financial advisers and bullying representatives of civil service agencies, whom he had trusted, but who had used the situation against him every time. We seemed to have become entrapped in a difficult situation and it seemed almost impossible to examine this kind of relationship without making him feel mocked or blamed. As long as he held on to his grievance, guilt was on the other side and he did not have to care about reparation.

Nevertheless, subsequently Mr. A. managed to recognise the characteristic repetitions of these constellations in his life and he found access to some, at times very sadistic thoughts of revenge, such as thoughts that his wife deserved to be tortured. To begin with, these thoughts were not accompanied by feelings of guilt. As a child, he had looked after injured animals on the duke's estate, while his brother went hunting with his father. Now, he began to discover that he had cruelly baited and tortured the objects who had disappointed him. This realisation enabled him to embark on psychoanalytic psychotherapy, which he had initially experienced as just another way of humiliating and violating him.

Discussion

For Mr. A., experiencing resentment was closely connected to a humiliating oedipal situation. He seemed to be identified with a weak, submissive father and his wife had chased him out of the role of 'the duke' by starting a relationship with another man. The cruelty of this situation was enacted in the first session, when he bowed deeply in front of me and I commented that he behaved just like his father for whom he felt contempt, which he experienced as another humiliation. In this moment, his hopefully raised gaze changed and he looked at me filled with hurt and accusation. This injury had to do with feeling excluded from a longed-for relationship, as had been the case with his wife, for whom everybody envied him. She had excluded him from an idealised relationship, had deceived him and humiliated him in an unbearable way.

Freud had already indicated that the disappointment of oedipal wishes was the cause of resentment when he characterised a type of patient who infers from a particular injustice experienced in early childhood that they are 'exceptions' entitling them 'to be spared any further demands' (Freud 1916d, p. 312). As a possible outcome of such humiliation, he saw the figure of the 'rebel', who derives 'pleasure (.) from the affliction of a weaker being (...) a pleasure due to masochistic satisfaction as well as to direct enjoyment' (Freud 1942a, p. 657).

Mr. A., too, had derived masochistic gratification from his humiliation and enacted such scenes in which he was put down and humiliated again and again. At the same time, he held on to his many psychosomatic complaints and seemed to derive some satisfaction from the failure of the people who treated him.

Among recent psychoanalytic authors who deal with complex defensive structures, Steiner (1993; 1996) describes resentment as a starting point for a pathological organisation of the personality. He demonstrates how an initially 'just cause', as in *Michael Kohlhaas*, is in due course taken over by destructive motives demanding revenge, thus making reconciliation difficult, as revenge is the opposite of reconciliation. Those who demand revenge cannot allow for reparation. In this transition from a wish for reparation to a need for revenge, *pride* seems to play a significant role (Steiner 1996), because pride makes the pursuit of reparation look like a renewed humiliation, and the hope that the counterpart will recognise their unfairness, have regrets and re-establish the original state will never be quite relinquished.

From a similar perspective, Michael Feldman (2008) showed how resentment can set in, in order to preserve oedipal constellations, not just including the 'near delusional possession of the object', but to protect the patient from shame, guilt and depressive pain (see Riesenberg-Malcolm & Roth 1999). For as long as resentment can be maintained, control over the object does not have to be given up. It is exactly this constellation which makes the overcoming of resentment so difficult and painful – a very desperate situation which underlies the impossibility of reparation.

> The feature of a grievance that I believe distinguishes it from a complaint [...] is the extent of the hostile, perverse gratification derived from the repetitive ruminations with which the grievance is nurtured. [...] the patient has a sense of injury, loss or deprivation that is unfair, unprovoked and unjust. [...] it seems as if analytic understanding is never adequate, never able to bring lasting relief or change. Patients may be gripped in a relentless way by a bitter, resentful feeling of deprivation, of being excluded from the place to which they feel entitled. Patients feel threatened by and indignant at any suggestion of further inquiry, particularly if that involves the examination of their own contribution to the situation that they feel aggrieved about, since that is not where they believe the problem lies. On the contrary, patients argue over and over that their object must change.
>
> (Feldman, 2008, p. 745)

The tenacity of holding on and the difficulty in overcoming those accusations which form the basis of the resentment seem to make reparation tremendously difficult. Conversely, chronic resentment can only be overcome when a willingness to forgive emerges and the efforts of reparation outweigh the wishes for revenge – a movement whose origins

Melanie Klein assumed to be in the early relationship to the parents, which she described as follows:

> If we have become able, deep in our unconscious minds, to clear our feelings to some extent towards our parents of grievances, and have forgiven them for the frustrations we had to bear, then we can be at peace with ourselves and are able to love others in the true sense of the word.
>
> (Klein 1937, p. 343)

However, the 'clearing' of our relationships of resentment takes an arduous and painful path. Because this makes leaving the retreat, which chronic resentment provides, inevitable and the feelings of guilt together with the wishes for revenge have to be faced.

> If the patient emerges from the retreat to face the current psychic reality he has to acknowledge that in phantasy he has attacked and destroyed his good objects in acts of vengeance that leave him and his objects devastated. Only then can he face the task of reconstructing his world and setting in motion the long and painful task of forgiveness and of making reparation.
>
> (Steiner, 1996, p. 436)

In a more recent contribution, Steiner (2018) points out that early trauma plays a significant role in the difficulties with reparation. Even Oedipus was a child rejected by his birth parents, abandoned and left to his fate.

Shame

In contrast to resentment, which is frequently not well hidden, shame is a dismal and mortifying affective state. Resentment can be a defence against feelings of shame and, vice versa, shame can give rise to resentment and wishes for revenge. Numerous authors have pointed out that shame is linked in a particular way to the experience of *being seen* (see Seidler 1995; Steiner 2006a; Küchenhoff 2007). The shamed one is faced by an observer who *watches* them critically and *looks down* on them. At times, the person is prepared to do anything just to avoid this demeaning experience.

Mr. A. was also plagued by feelings of shame. For example, he felt that he could only go to his restaurant secretly at night, so as not to be seen by anybody. On the way to treatment, he was worried by the idea that he might bump into former patrons and they would talk to him. And in therapy it was torture for him to have to wait for the sessions. He suspected that I always deliberately started something else, came too early or too late, opened the windows or closed them to make the heating rattle, moved the couch minimally in order to make him react and then interpret that reaction. Just lying on the couch was experienced as a humiliation by him. And in some of my interventions he heard a sneering undertone, which confirmed to him that I said what I said with the intention of 'making him feel small' and to further humiliate him.

Originally in psychoanalytic literature, shame was linked to the uncovering of that which one wants to keep concealed, namely being naked, being exposed and being humiliated. Accordingly, Freud (1896b, 1916–17a) describes shame as a *defensive motive* and emphasises its relation to *scopophilia* (Freud 1905d). At the same time he takes note of the absence of shame in certain mental conditions, such as exhibitionism or the self-accusations of melancholics. From the latter he concludes that 'one part of the ego sets itself over against the other, judges it critically, and, as it were, takes it as its object' (Freud, 1916–17g, p. 432).

Following on from Freud, there was a delay in theorising about shame, despite its clinical relevance and in contrast to other complex affective states (see Weiss 2015c). Between 1910 and 1940, there are very few papers explicitly dealing with the topic of shame (Friedjung 1913; Eisler 1919; Spielrein 1920; Nunberg 1932), as if understanding the role of guilt in neurotic conflicts was of predominant importance.

Only from the 1950s onward did an increasing theoretical and clinical interest in the meaning of shame begin to emerge. A number of publications dealt with the relationship between shame and guilt (Piers & Singer 1953; Levin 1967; Lewis 1971; Wurmser 1981), while other authors were interested in the significance of shame in the development of identity (Lynd 1958; Thrane 1979) and its role in early narcissistic states (Kohut 1966; 1968; Grunberger 1971; Broucek 1982; Morrison 1983; 1989).

Developmental aspects of the psychology of shame were taken up variously (Erikson 1959; Schore 1991), their significance in the development of object relations was picked up (Spero 1984), as well as investigating their function in unconscious phantasy systems (Rizzuto 1991). In a survey paper from 1994, Melvin Lansky speaks of a 'veritable explosion of interest in shame' (p. 433) since the 1970s.

With the increasing clinical significance of narcissistic and borderline pathologies, the relationship between shame, ego-ideal and super-ego became a central focus (Miller 1985; Rothstein 1994; Wurmser 2003).

Leon Wurmser (1981; 1987) investigated the role of shame in various super-ego pathologies and spoke about a 'dilemma' between shame and guilt. With this he refers to the paradoxical situation of shame being used to 'mask' guilt on the one hand, but also being covered up by feelings of guilt under different conditions. He showed, furthermore, how shame can be cloaked in manifold ways as contempt, mockery, defiance and anger. In a recent paper (Wurmser 2015) he speaks of a 'tragic circularity' of severe trauma, chronic shame and repetitive self-harm.

This way of seeing shame uncovers the whole ambiguity about it (see Nathanson 1987; Sas 1992), in as much as it is a protection of the self as well as being a source of humiliation and abasement. At times, this provides a retreat where the underlying grandiosity, envy and feelings of guilt can be hidden (Steiner 1993). Occasionally *hidden shame* is an impediment to the working through of feelings of guilt. In this way, shame can hinder movements towards reparation and forgiveness, as pointed out by Melvin Lansky (2001; 2005) among other authors. Together with its relationship to envy and to the 'evil eye' (Wurmser 1991), shame becomes a possible source of *negative therapeutic reactions*. Riccardo Lombardi (2007) pointed out the primitive bodily and psychotic representations of shame. It may, therefore, make sense to distinguish between *depressive* and *paranoid-schizoid shame* analogous to depressive and paranoid-schizoid guilt.

Just as being overwhelmed by shame, the absence of shame can be an indication of a pathological personality organisation. In this context, Claude Janin (2007; 2015) talks about 'white shame' *(honte blanche)* denoting such states as he has observed in hatred and in an increased use of pornography. In such cases, regaining the capacity for shame would constitute therapeutic progress.

Over and above the specific area of psychopathology, shame has of course always been a classic subject matter of religion, mythology, philosophy, literature and culture (see Lewis 1987). The work of Seidler (1995), Demmerling & Landweer (2007) as well as Küchenhoff et al. (2013) provide an overview of this. Indeed, from Aristotle to Sartre (1943) there is a long tradition of thinking about shame long before this aroused the interest of psychoanalysts as a clinical phenomenon. However, it was left to the latter to examine its unconscious sources and dynamics. In this way, psychoanalysis not only contributed to the clarification of individual shame, but also provided important approaches to the understanding of shame in political, socio-cultural and historic contexts (see Steinberg 1991; Lansky & Morrison 1997; Wurmser 2004; 2015; Hollan 2012).

One aspect, which I see as particularly seminal, is the relation of shame to the experience of seeing and being seen, which I will go on to explore with examples of recent developments within the Kleinian tradition.

In contrast to ego- and self-psychology, shame as an organised affective state became the subject of closer inspection relatively late in the development of Kleinian thinking. Herbert Rosenfeld (1987) drew attention to the role of humiliation and Ruth Riesenberg-Malcolm (1970) described in a detailed case study how the fantasy of observing cruel and shameful sexual acts in a mirror served one of her female patients as a protection from a psychotic breakdown. In her patient, the eyes functioned as a means by which the objects could be penetrated behind the mirror. On the other hand, seeing was also an attempt to hold the scene together and protect her ego from fragmentation.

A comprehensive exploration of shame was provided by John Steiner (2006a; 2011a). He sketched out a spectrum of feelings of shame ranging from mild forms of shyness, embarrassment, bashfulness to demeaning experiences of humiliation, denigration and abasement. In his view, the patient is most exposed to feelings of shame when they leave the protection of their narcissistic retreat and face up to the experience of being seen.

In his work on 'scopophilia', Otto Fenichel took up Melanie Klein's (1932; 1946) ideas of projective and introjective processes as early as 1935. He coined the phrase 'ocular introjection' and demonstrated that in particular conditions, seeing is in the service of excitable, possessive and engulfing motives which have in common the aim to eliminate *the separateness from the object*. Mr. A., whose gesture of humility was described above, spoke in this context of his 'sucking gaze'. The 'sucking' mostly served to take in the idealised characteristics of his counterpart, in order not to have to feel shame, envy and painful separateness. In this way, seeing becomes equivalent to other 'early' sense modalities: taste, smell, feel and touch, which do not know genuine separateness. However, the experience of the gaze is different from other sense modalities in that it introduces the experience of distance. Seeing always implies *a distance to the other,* just as *being seen* confronts us with the *experience of their otherness.* Jean-Paul Sartre (1943) placed this break in one's own subjectivity by the gaze of the other in the centre of his phenomenological analysis of intersubjectivity.

According to Steiner, the experience of the gaze is therefore probably the earliest *representation of a third.* As the baby sucks at the mother's breast, their gazes meet and thus the dimension of *meaning* comes into play. The contact between mouth and breast is thereby broadened and deepened. This makes the mother not just the object of desire, but an observing figure, who introduces something new and unexpected into the contact.

The experience of the gaze and its bearing on the exchange of phantasies between mother and child has been emphasised by various psychoanalytic authors. But while writers such as Donald Winnicott (1967) or Jacques Lacan (1949)[1] stress the mirroring aspect, Steiner attends to the reciprocal character of being looked at. Just as the baby expresses its emotional state and seeks the attention of the mother, her gaze in turn conveys her emotional state which might mean joy or validation, disapproval or rejection, alarm or accusation. The experience of being seen is thus unavoidably linked in with the experience of self-consciousness, embarrassment and shame.[2] It goes hand in hand with the transition from part-object experiences to whole-object relations, because seeing and being seen inevitably means being perceived as a *whole person* with good as well as bad characteristics.

The complexity of this relationship is increased by the presence of the father, who disrupts the unity of mother and child who only have eyes for each other. He introduces the perception of the parental couple into the closeness of the mother-child-relationship, which can arouse feelings of smallness, exclusion and inferiority, all of which can be conveyed through the gaze. When this becomes unbearable, the *direction of the gaze can be reverted,* and the eye can now be used to penetrate the other, discover their weaknesses and expose them in turn to humiliation and indignity.

Karl Abraham (1913) in his paper on 'Restitutions and transformations of scopophilia in psychoneurotics' remarked that in certain cases 'the person ascribes some kind of virtue to his eye or his glance as though he were in possession of magic powers' (p. 199). The gaze is then in the service of 'omnipotence' and the eye becomes a 'sadistic weapon' (p. 200). Steiner (2006a) and Segal (2007) have pointed out how looking can be used in this way to get rid of unbearable feelings by putting them into others.

The notion of the eye as an active organ with the power to influence the person looked at by sending out 'rays' has been familiar since antiquity, in particular in the context of 'the evil eye' (see Jahn 1855, p. 32; Rakoczy 1996; Haubl 2001, p. 67). Although envy has been identified as the main source of 'the evil eye', it is not solely envious feelings which are put into the other. Other emotional states, such as joy, anxiety, anger or sadness can also be transmitted in this way. When dealing with humiliation and abasement, this tendency to project will be all the keener, the mightier the quest for superiority and the more pronounced the feeling of shame experienced. By this *projective use of the gaze* the individual can attempt to regain a narcissistic position from which he/she feels expelled. The motives for this inversion of direction are manifold. They can hide feelings of inferiority, turn shame into triumph or intrude into the idealised object in order to find a hiding place within them. What all these motives have in common is that they eliminate separateness in order to re-establish a narcissistic object relationship.

At times, one's own readiness to shame and belittle others is projected. And it is frequently this tendency, which makes the details of the analytic setting, such as the coming and going at pre-arranged times, the lying on the couch, the exclusion from the analyst's personal life, their capacity to observe and understand, into something unbearable. It can then be difficult to interpret shame without exposing the patient to renewed humiliation. The following vignette will illustrate some of these difficulties.

Clinical vignette

Mrs. B., a 35-year-old librarian had come to analysis because of insecurity, agonising self-doubts and recurrent depressive episodes. For a long time, she had idealised the relationship with me. After a certain point, however, the same thing that plagued her elsewhere in her life was repeated and she experienced my interpretations now as humiliating and demeaning. Similarly to Mr. A., she presumed that I used my position to show her my superiority.

The initial idealisation was mirrored among other things by her parking her car in an area which I also used and which was reserved for hospital staff. She feared that she would be caught by someone controlling the car park, and she took various measures to protect herself. For instance, she put a note on her windscreen saying 'Please understand!'. I thought, she feared that I might find out that she had gained unauthorised access to my internal world, and would be cast out when she transgressed the limits of my 'understanding'.

After exploring different versions of this situation and coming to a closer understanding of it, Mrs. B. could use the public car park of the clinic which was accessible for everyone. But this was accompanied by new complaints about the blocking barrier, queues going in and out of the car park, the required car park fee, the registration of the time by the car park meter, etc. She seemed to experience these situations, and particularly my interpretations in regard of these, as humiliating and made me responsible for it.

One day, she arrived to her session in an agitated state and described in great detail a situation of following a car on her way to the clinic. Suddenly, the window on the driver's side opened and a carelessly chucked out banana peel landed on her radiator. Indignant, she followed the car and caught up next to the car at the crossroads at a red traffic light. At eye level with the driver of the car, she gesticulated angrily through the closed window at him, who seemed to wonder about her behaviour and followed her to the clinic to ask her why she was so agitated. Curtly, she responded whether he found it all right to chuck a banana peel in front of her car. He said very calmly 'And this is why you are so agitated?'. Once again, she felt mocked and humiliated by such a response.

In the following sessions, it emerged that during this time, Mrs. B. frequently experienced my interpretations like throwing banana peels in front of her to make her slip up. Then, I would look down on her from my superior position observing her in her pitiful situation, commenting serenely on her indignant reaction. She hated these 'banana-peel-interpretations' as she called them, and tried to avoid such situations, by getting at eye level with me and sending angry warning looks. In so doing, she sometimes got me to give my interpretations in a slightly overcautious and guarded way, as if I wanted to avoid confrontation and not become that patronising figure, who shames and humiliates her.

The subsequent long phase of her analysis was characterised by the painful insight that she herself too often thought she was superior to others and in her fantasies tended to humiliate and demean them. She was shocked when she discovered that such thoughts were sometimes directed against me, as she liked me and was grateful for our co-operation. The realisation of her hatred confronted her with feelings of guilt, which seemed almost unbearable to her at times. She had been protected from them for as long as she could project them into others and felt ashamed being confronted by them.

During this difficult time, I was late one morning as I had got stuck in a traffic jam. I asked the secretary to inform Mrs. B., who was already waiting. When I arrived, just short of fifteen minutes late, she noticed my haste and embarrassment. She asked me in a friendly way whether I needed a bit more time, but then started the session immediately.

While there may have been a touch of superiority in her equanimity observing me rushing in, her reaction to my lateness was palpably different from those of previous situations, when her having to wait would have been experienced as shameful and provocative. She had also reacted with gratitude to the secretary giving her my message, when in the past she would have seen it as belittling that I 'sent' the secretary after her as I thought of her as so little, sick and dependent that she could not wait on her own for a few minutes. This altered attitude seemed to be linked to a greater acceptance of the oedipal situation, where she did no longer feel so small and worthless between me and the secretary. I limited myself in this session to interpret her changed attitude which had allowed her to forgive my lateness and to experience the presence of the secretary as caring. Mrs. B. had noticed this change herself and added that there was a moment when she saw me and asked whether I needed a minute, in which she felt superior and gleeful about my lateness.

Discussion

I think this situation reflected Mrs. B.'s increased capacity to think about her feelings. Instead of feeling shamed by an object who looks down on her, she now felt freer to explore her own occasional contemptuous thoughts. This transition was related to her acknowledgement of her feelings of guilt, which in turn got her in touch with her affection for me and her concurrent hatred of me. Grappling with these emotions enabled her to have a more open and direct relationship in which feelings of shame and being seen receded into the background. She felt less forced to put these feelings into me, could adopt a more conciliatory attitude towards my lateness, so that we could see 'eye to eye' despite the asymmetry of the analytic situation. In this position, she was able to accept my interventions, without immediately feeling insulted and humiliated.

On the relationship of guilt and shame, Ronald Britton (1989; 1997) formulated the idea that guilt characterises the relationship to the primary object, *the object of desire,* while shame characterises the relationship to the *observing object.* Steiner (2002, p. 105; 2006a) took up this idea and emphasised that humiliation and shame are frequently powerful impediments to the working through of feelings of guilt, because the working through of guilt requires *time,* while humiliation and shame call for speedy relief (Steiner 2015; see Riesenberg-Malcolm & Roth 1999). This urgent presence of shame, in contrast to guilt, which presupposes a relation to something that has already happened, is also highlighted in recent phenomenological studies. Sonja Rinofner-Kreidl (2012) points out the moment of *being paralysed* during the experience of shame and emphasises, like Dan Zahavi (2013), the *unavoidable alterity* which forms the basis of the experience of shame, insofar as another is always involved.

The following schematic diagram (Figure 2) sketches out the relationship between guilt and shame:

This perspective presupposes the working through of shame as a precondition for the recognition of guilt. Only when the patient is able to face the experience of shame is it possible to proceed from feelings of shame, humiliation and bitterness to a confrontation with feelings of guilt, which facilitate the process of mourning and reparation (Klein 1937; 1940) and therefore steps towards genuine forgiveness (Rey, 1986).

In treatment, the therapist becomes the object of desire as well as being the observing object of the oedipal relationship. Split parts of the self can be projected into either, so that the analyst may be turned into a narcissistically exploitative, voyeuristically excitable or cruelly observing figure. It is precisely this constellation which makes it so difficult to interpret shame and humiliation without exposing the patient to the very situation they

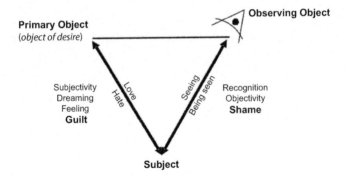

Figure 2 Shame and guilt in their relationship to the object of desire and the observing object (after Britton 1989; 1997, Steiner 2002, in: Weiss & Frank 2002, Steiner 2006a)

unconsciously fear most. At times, feelings of guilt get stirred up in the therapist, which have to be worked through to enable the patient to withdraw their projections, because the analyst too can be hampered by too much shame and guilt (or a lack thereof) in gaining a deeper understanding, which is necessary to get processes of reparation going (see Steiner 2015).

Rage and wrath

Unlike resentment and shame, rage is a feeling in which the individual looks down on others in condemnation. Rage has been called 'the wrath of the gods', and it is an angry god who chains Prometheus to the Caucasian rocks. Aristotle denoted anger (ὀργή) as revenge for a slight 'by someone who is not entitled to slight'. Wrath shares the relationship to fire with resentment. But unlike resentment, which 'smoulders' and turns into something chronic, wrath 'flares up' and destroys (just as lightning 'strikes' and the rolling thunder 'resonates'). Because of its destructive force, in antiquity authors already referred to it as the 'worst of all affects' (see Hühn 2004; Walde 2004).

The raging of anger and its destructive influence on human relations was clearly seen by philosophers of antiquity, such as Seneca[3] or the stoics. For this reason, a borderline patient did not dare look other people in the eye when in a state of anger. She experienced her eyes as 'flame-throwers' and feared to 'set alight' her counterpart.

The gaze of the wrathful one is from *above to below*. This lends it strength and superiority. In the theological tradition, wrath is a privilege of God and linked to the attribute of 'holiness'. In Greek mythology the wrath of the gods is understood as retaliation which 'restores damaged order' (Maurer 2004, p. 1390). As long as it is used as a punishment, wrath is 'just': it does not gain its strength from the protest against injustice (like grievance), but from the *certainty of being right.* This is from where it derives its violence, which does not tolerate doubt or contradiction.

Other authors, such as the Epicurean Philodemos of Gadara[4], distinguished different graduations of anger and wrath. While 'mild anger' could still be reconciled with wisdom, 'bad anger' leads to a disconnection from reason. Maybe, analogous to shame, there is a continuum of feelings of anger, ranging from 'just reluctance' (νέμεσις)[5], via protest, indignation, outrage and contempt to 'holy wrath' as well as to destructive attacks on thinking (see Bion 1959).

In contrast to the philosophical tradition, where wrath and its relation to morality has been a central topic from antiquity to the present time (Demmerling & Landweer 2007, p. 287), psychoanalysis has not widely explored wrath, anger and rage as discreet, organised emotional states. Kernberg (2004) assigns rage and anger to the destructive impulses. Wurmser (1981; 1987) mentions anger in relation to feelings of resentment and vengeance. Only the work of Eric Brenman (1985) and Irma Brenman Pick (1993) are exceptions to this. Brenman Pick distinguishes 'healthy protest' from destructive rage, which can manifest itself in different ways. In her view, the 'wrathful super-ego' is derived from a lack of 'containment' in early life under the influence of cruelty and rejection.

In Sophocles' *Oedipus on Colonus,* Steiner (1990) describes wrath as an emotional transition from guilt to omnipotence. De Masi (1997) explores wrath in relation to the psychotic super-ego, which according to his view, spreads terror rather than guilt. With reference to the perverse object relationship, he suggests that every perverse system resorts to 'hyper morality', which is ultimately directed against life and development (De Masi 1989, p. 428). Frank (2015a) has drawn attention to the 'annihilating look' and its significance in super-ego pathology, and Freud (1926d) saw wrath as a 'punishment of the super-ego'.

One possible reason that wrath has received such astonishingly little attention as an independent, organised affective state in psychoanalysis might be that it frequently occurs in concealed fashion. Because, similarly to the experience of envy (Klein 1957), anxiety about its destructive effects can be very pronounced. In this case, complex defence strategies come into play, which turn wrath and rage into chronic forms of moaning, self-contempt and bitterness. Not infrequently the wrathful gaze is projected, which gives rise to the conviction of being condemned by an idealised, morally superior figure.

Clinical vignette

Mr. C., a 35-year-old religious education teacher, referred himself because of chronic feelings of failure together with depressive symptoms and numerous physical ailments. He attributed these symptoms to his 'weak character' and hoped that therapy could free him from these. Despite his social engagement and his affectionate sides, which were evident in his relationship with his wife and young son, he continuously bemoaned his shortcomings and often reacted with irritation to affection and closeness. He strived for an attitude of moral superiority, which was supposed to relieve him of any addiction and libidinal drives.

This ideal seemed to be linked to an uncle in whose family the patient had grown up. His parents had separated very early on and, because of a congenital handicap, he had not been able to adequately take his mother's milk. There were hints that this had reinforced the mother's chronic unhappiness and had formed the basis of his later feelings of guilt. The uncle was a member of a sect-like organised Christian minority, whose rigid belief principles shaped family life. Very early in life, Mr. C. had developed the feeling that he could not live up to these requirements. He experienced his needs as moral weakness and traced them back to his lack of belief. Mr. C. met his professional duties with great seriousness, but here, too, saw his expectation of failure confirmed by the occasional criticism of pupils and colleagues, which left him feeling he had chosen the 'wrong profession'.

In his analysis, too, Mr. C. frequently appeared to deal with a superior figure who looked down on him contemptuously. He saw himself as a 'hopeless case' and wondered why I had taken him on. Either, so he thought, I was particularly naïve in my hope of being able to help him or else I was totally indifferent to him and only interested in my scientific research.

Mr. C. often seemed withdrawn and bitter. But sometimes he brought dreams, and there were sessions when a warmer emotional contact developed. When I commented on this, he usually withdrew quickly and called me over-confident in my 'false hope', as if he needed to put an end to any prospect of change. In one of these sessions, for instance, he had talked movingly about his sadness at the funeral of his grandfather. He looked as abandoned and helpless as a little boy. Towards the end of the session, however, his mood shifted and he left with a pastoral, regretful gaze as though we had just buried our work together and he wanted to give me his condolences with his handshake.

It was mostly at weekends when he lost contact and withdrew contritely. He wanted to be 'left alone', to prepare his lessons and reacted irritably and angrily towards his family. Sometimes it could happen that he had completely forgotten the content of the session by the following Monday. Nevertheless, his withdrawal could gradually be better understood. Behind his bitterness and self-accusations, an internal organisation built on angers slowly emerged. It was based on a moral system which judged reality not on *how it was*, but *how it should be*.

This moralistic organisation included a number of fundamentalist convictions. In particular, Mr. C. believed that the analysis provided a superior belief system, which would deliver him of his weaknesses if he suffered it long enough. Furthermore, he believed that 'truth was hell'. When his needy sides were addressed, he sometimes reacted contemptuously by referring to the treatment as 'wellness'. On occasion, he could feel his rage flare up and he became afraid of his own destructiveness. In these flare-ups, he seemed to be identified with a *wrathful god*, who looked down on the life of humans. On the other hand, his wish for support and contact became clearly palpable.

In a dream towards the end of the second year of his analysis, Mr. C. walked across a frozen lake with his little son. In their curiosity, they had walked out too far into the lake following a bird which was diving for food in an ice-free spot. At this moment, the ice broke. He and his son had to fight for their lives, swimming back to shore through the cold water.

I interpreted that his curiosity had led him further into the analysis than he had originally intended. Now his frozen internal world showed cracks, and like the bird, he was perhaps hoping to find some nourishment in our sessions. However, this meant to be dependent on help and like father and son, he had to swim with me through cold water.

For a moment Mr. C. seemed to be touched by my comment. He said nothing for a while and seemed close to tears. After a short pause, he regained his composure and remembered that his uncle had told him the story of Jesus and the fishermen on the lake of Galilee. If the belief was strong enough, his uncle had explained to him, one could walk on water.

Discussion

I initially understood Mr. C.'s comment as containing a recognition of the omnipotence of his existing belief system. He seemed to be touched by my interpretation. But it was ultimately unclear whether this, just as the story of his uncle, was just another pious story to him.

This movement away from emotional contact back to his world of religious and moralistic beliefs was characteristic for Mr. C., and often occurred when he got in touch with feelings of helplessness and neediness. In fact, he often questioned the analysis when progress became evident in the sessions. This could happen in different ways: for instance, by extracting the emotional substance from my interpretations, a process, which he compared with the chemical reaction of 'sedimentation' of protein particles from a nutrient solution. In this way, he turned my interpretations into little 'super-ego-lumps' devoid of anything nourishing, which he could then use like commandments, to which he had to submit. In such moments, his gaze seemed to be directed contemptuously towards himself and he withdrew into humility and 'contrition'. However, if he became more conscious of his wrath, he could be overwhelmed by shame and feelings of guilt. At such times, he could hardly bear to see his face in the mirror.

However painful these experiences were for the patient, they allowed him step by step to get closer to his mourning and feelings of guilt hidden behind his anger. Because as long as he was angry, he could not feel genuine regret. Wrath does not allow for reparation. It can only be *placated*. This is the reason why the gaze of the wrathful one remains directed from above to below even when granting *mercy* to the counterpart.

Summary

In my reflections, I have tried to differentiate the narcissistic states of resentment, shame and wrath by *the direction of the gaze*. While the gaze is directed from below to above in an accusatory way in resentment, the shamed one sees him/herself faced with an object, which looks down on them in a humiliating way. In contrast, in rage and wrath the gaze is directed from above to below. The individual assumes a superior position, from which he/she is judgemental and condemnatory.

All three states of mind frequently develop on a background of early privation and traumatic experiences. They can become the source of pathological organisations of the personality (Steiner 1993), promoting the withdrawal into states of psychic retreat and thus hindering psychic development and change. I have tried to show various defensive movements within these states. This can lead to a reversal of the direction of the gaze. The eye is then used to project cruelty, guilt or worthlessness into the other. There are also transitions between resentment, shame and wrath. Thus, for instance, resentment can turn into wrath by way of revenge, whereby the individual shifts from a subordinate to a superior position.

What all three states have in common is that resentment, shame and wrath serve in different ways to avoid feelings of guilt. Conflicts of mourning and guilt are circumvented and the way towards reparation is blocked. In resentment, it is the wish for retaliation and revenge which impedes reparation. Shame is experienced as an injury to pride and engenders the need to reverse the situation and shame others. Finally, wrath only allows for reparation in the form of mercy granted from a morally superior position.

Particularly in wrath, the defensive formations have been little investigated so far. I have attempted to describe humility, idealisation and contrition as positions that hide rage and wrath. More than resentment and shame, in which 'fairness' and trauma play an important role, wrath seems to be based on fundamentalist convictions (Britton 1998). This lends the enraged one moral superiority, but is at the same time linked with severe anxiety about the destructive effects of their wrath.

In the following chapter, the ramifications of resentment and wrath on the self and its impeding effect on processes of reparation will be explored in more detail with a clinical case presentation. I will examine the role of the super-ego more closely as a structure, which can either facilitate of hinder processes of reparation.

Notes

1 'What does the baby see when he or she looks at the mother's face? I am suggesting that, ordinarily, what the baby sees is himself or herself' Winnicott (1971): 'The Mirror-role of Mother and Family in Child Development' (in *Playing and Reality*). Lacan (1949) also describes in his theory the mirroring stage of the gaze as a paradigm of a narcissistic object relationship. However, he emphasises, akin to Bion's (1962) model of containment, its function in eliminating experiences of fragmentation of the imaginary constitution of the subject *(image du corps morcelé)* (see Weiss & Pagel 1995).
2 Some findings in the research on the mirroring of affect or affect resonance in early child development point in the same direction, although they do so without specific reference to the genesis of the feelings of shame (see Stern 1985; Gergely & Watson 1996; Fonagy et al. 2003). Stern (1985) in particular pointed out the central significance of the gaze in the evolution of intersubjectivity.
3 See Seneca, *De Ira*, I, 1, 1; II, 12, 6
4 See Philodemos, *De Ira Liber* (published by T. Gomperz). Leipzig 1864: Teubner
5 See Aristoteles, *Rhetorik*, 1386b, 112.2

Chapter 3

Repetition compulsion and the primitive super-ego

Attempts at reparation in borderline patients

Love, guilt and reparation are seen as the necessary counterparts to those aggressive impulses which result from the dependency on our first love objects (see Klein & Rivière 1937). When they converge, regret, sorrow and endeavours at reparation emerge at the very moments when the damage done to the object, real or in phantasy, can no longer be denied and feelings of guilt arise in order to avert the loss of the love object and protect it from further damage.

Such developments become possible when persecutory anxieties recede and splits are overcome, so that the individual makes the experience that feelings of love and hate are directed against the *same person*. Now the individual does not feel as persecuted by bad figures as before and at the same time discovers that it is his/her own aggressive impulses which may endanger his/her most important relationships. This discovery evokes a critical situation, as the child now has to live with the fear of having damaged the beloved object and perhaps of losing it forever. Melanie Klein (1935; 1940; 1946) referred to this very transition as the entry to the depressive position. Now it is not so much persecutory anxieties and the struggle for one's own survival, but feelings of mourning and guilt which come to the fore. They go hand in hand with the worry about the loss of the love object. When the pain related to these feelings becomes too great, renewed tendencies for splitting and withdrawal can be deployed. It is then still the same person whose affection one longs for and against whom one feels resentment and grievance, but it is now two versions of the same relationship which coexist seemingly without contradiction so that feelings of guilt and the need for reparation can be evaded.

Reparation can be regarded as an elementary process which counteracts destruction and disintegration, as described in Chapter 1. Hanna Segal (1952; 1957; 1981; 1991) has shown in her work that, in the depressive position processes of reparation are closely related to processes of symbolisation; because it is only through symbolisation that it becomes possible to mourn a loss and to re-create the lost, damaged object internally as a good object, for it to be available in situations of absence. The capacity to endure separation and to create new meaning and life is thus closely bound up with successful reparation. The starting point for Segal's deliberations were Klein's discoveries from her observations in child analyses, where, working with small children, she could directly experience the interrelation between damage, reparation and the emergence of processes of symbolisation in the children's play activities, their verbal utterances and their drawings (Klein 1932; Frank 2009; 2012).

But how are these processes fashioned in patients who are only transiently or partially capable of such integration? Can we trace here, too, movements in the direction of the depressive position? How are these primitive reparative attempts constructed and how do they affect the analytic situation? These questions are the concern of this chapter.

Precursors of processes of reparation in psychotic, obsessive-compulsive, narcissistic and borderline patients

One of the first authors to investigate processes of reparation in great detail was Henry Rey (1986), who described the precursors of such movements even in schizoid and borderline patients. He regarded reparation as a universal process serving the maintenance and renewal of the organism.

Following on from Freud (1911c), he pointed out that, based on clinical observations, even schizophrenic patients make attempts at restitution of their fragmented internal world by creating a new, albeit bizarre, reality. These delusional constructions serve as a protection and retreat, and in this wider sense they can be understood as desperate attempts to protect the self from further dissolution and fragmentation at the price of losing contact with reality.

In his paper 'The loss of reality in neurosis and psychosis', Freud (1924e) discerned two steps, the first of which 'would drag the ego away (…) from reality, while the second would try to make good the damage done' (pp. 183–184). Differently to neurosis where it is 'at the expense of a restriction of the id', in psychosis this happens 'in another, more autocratic manner, by the creation of a new reality' (ibid.). What both pathologies have in common, is that they constitute an 'attempt at reparation'.

However, the psychotic attempt at restitution turns out quite differently, although it may involve elements of manic or even genuine reparation (see Bronstein 2016). Unlike neurotic, narcissistic and borderline attempts at reparation, it consolidates the fundamental break in the relationship with the external world. In contrast, attempts at reparation in non-psychotic patients are predominantly located in the patient's internal world.

In this way, *obsessive-compulsive rituals* can be understood as an attempt to magically restore an object which has been damaged by sadistic attacks and has possibly become vengeful. As Freud (1909d) already described, these precautions serve mainly to avert internal threats (instinctual desires) under the dominance of a cruel super-ego. Other motives may be that they provide *preventive measures,* to protect from anxieties of punishment and loss. Obsessive-compulsive symptoms offer to some degree *control* over the object, but do not allow for a real working through of separation and guilt. The significance of the ruminations and the doubts, the compulsive ambivalence based on the quest to 'dominate the object' has been pointed out by Abraham (1924, see Abraham 1913). Ines Sodré (1994) could furthermore show that obsessional doubt and obsessional certainty obstruct the acknowledgement of the oedipal situation, i.e. the recognition of the differences between the generations and the sexes.

Resentment and *grievance* are further clinically relevant constellations, where the patient while unremittingly demanding reparation, keeps the wounds open and ultimately does not permit reparation. In the previous chapter, I have tried to show that resentment can be understood as a state in which the need for reparation is projected and therefore recurs as an insatiable demand for reparation, which cannot be stilled. What is denied here is the transition from the need for revenge to a wish for settlement and conciliation.

We come across *manic forms of reparation* mainly in narcissistic and borderline patients (see Klein 1935; Winnicott 1935). They show signs of 'attack is the best form of defence', wanting to quickly get rid of guilt, but actually bringing about renewed harm and damage of the object time and again. The god-like magnificence of Oedipus on Colonus (Steiner 1990) or the grandiosity of King Lear (Rusbridger 2011) are examples of this. In less pronounced forms of manic reparation, it can occasionally be difficult to distinguish between genuine reparation and pseudo-versions of reparation. Sometimes, elements of denial, wanting to undo things and genuine reparation seem to exist side by side.

When we look closely at the *self-harming* of some borderline patients, they too can be seen to some extent as concrete attempts at reparation. Not only do they serve as a relief from unbearable internal tension, but as a form of self-punishment defending against mourning and guilt (see Riesenberg-Malcolm 1981). In this way, aggression can be bound and psychic pain can be turned into physical pain. As long as this dynamic is not understood, the patient can possibly be robbed of the only means of defence they possess against damaging their internal objects by measures

of sanctions and control. Maybe Oedipus blinding himself after the discovery of being guilty of his father's death and the suicide of his mother is
an example of this (see Steiner 1985).

In comparing these primitive antecedents with more mature forms of
reparation, one notices that they *perpetuate* in one way or another *the
damage to the object* and thus result in these never-ending cycles of
unconscious guilt, repetition and negative therapeutic reaction, which
Freud described in his papers 'The economic problem of masochism'
(Freud 1924c) and 'Analysis terminable and interminable' (Freud 1937c).
When such a vicious circle has been established, then certain manifestations of the repetition compulsion can possibly be understood as desperate and recurrently failing attempts at reparation. In some ways, these
patients resemble those figures from Greek mythology (Sisyphus, Prometheus, Tantalus), whose rebellion against the gods, the primitive
super-ego, led to endless torture and punishment. A closer understanding of successful and failing reparation therefore has to take into
account the relationship of processes of reparation and the super-ego.

Attempts at reparation and the development of the super-ego

This addresses the role of the super-ego in the success or failure of
processes of reparation. In the following, I would like to examine those
procedures which enable reparation and those which block this development permanently. In this, I will start with Melanie Klein's thesis
that *it is the evolution of the super-ego structures which makes reparation possible, while under the dominance of an archaic super-ego the
damage is endlessly perpetuated.*

Klein has presented her thoughts on this in her paper 'On the
development of mental functioning' (1958). In this paper, she shows
how the early, archaic super-ego originates by the splitting off of
destructive parts of the ego. In this early stage, it serves as a kind of
bad bank, in which primitive, destructive impulses together with persecutory projections which threaten the integrity of the ego can be
stored. However, as this rudimentary super-ego structure is always also
influenced by elements of the life instinct and loving experiences, it
gradually changes its character and can in the further course of development relate to the ego in a facilitating way. Klein remarks on this:

> As the process of integration goes on (…), the death instinct is
> bound, up to a point, by the super-ego (…) with the result that the
> action of the super-ego ranges from restraint of hate and

destructive impulses, protection of the good object and self-criticism, to threats, inhibitory complaints and persecution.

(Klein 1958, p. 240)

If the preservative qualities predominate, the sadistic traits of the super-ego fade into the background. While the primitive super-ego poses an enduring threat to the ego, the developing super-ego can increasingly take on a containment function for the ego. Klein recognised this intrapsychic *function of containment* of the super-ego towards the ego when she emphasised that 'the super-ego – being bound up with the good object and even striving for its preservation comes close to the actual good mother' (ibid., p. 240) who cares and protects the child from threats and primitive persecutory anxieties.

The imposition of privations and prohibitions continues to be part of the functions of this super-ego, which, however, is no longer directed in a sadistic way against the ego. As Melanie Klein put it: 'To some extent, when development goes well, the super-ego is largely felt as helpful and does not operate as too harsh a conscience'. One of its functions now is to 'to protect the good object' (ibid., p. 240).

What Klein describes here is the evolution of the super-ego from a *bad bank* to a *container* and ultimately to an agency that facilitates reparation in the ego. The development of the ego functions goes hand in hand with this and is accompanied by an increasing acceptance of the super-ego by the ego, sharing 'different aspects of the same good object' (ibid.). Klein summarises:

> With the strengthening of the ego and its growing capacity for integration and synthesis, the stage of the depressive position is reached. At this stage the injured object is no longer predominantly felt as a persecutor but as a loved object towards whom a feeling of guilt and the urge to make reparation are experienced.
>
> (ibid., pp. 241–242)

Klein's approach specifically emphasises the idea of the *evolution of super-ego structures* closely connected to the development or blockade of ego functions. This is linked to the idea that the primitive super-ego structures exist throughout life alongside the mature super-ego and that there is a permanent interchange between the primitive and mature super-ego, just as between the ego and the super-ego. Depending on how this exchange is formed, different constellations can develop, which either facilitate steps towards reparation or lead to an enduring status quo, perpetuating damage of the internal objects with a corresponding impairment of ego functions (see Riesenberg-Malcolm 1987; O'Shaughnessy 1999).

Processes which facilitate or systematically impede reparation

In the following section, the processes blocking genuine reparation and thus leading to continuous damage of the internal objects will be investigated by using clinical material from the analysis of a borderline patient. As I have tried to show, primitive attempts at reparation are distinguished from mature steps mainly by:

- remaining relatively concrete
- serving primarily the control of anxiety
- the impossibility of real acknowledgement of separateness and
- a mere pseudo-acceptance of reality

Nevertheless, they are successful to some degree, as they lead at least temporarily to a relief from anxiety and unbearable guilt. But they get stuck halfway, so to say, as the experience of loss is circumvented and the control of the object cannot be relinquished. Sometimes, this can lead to desperate situations, in which the individual remains forever encased with their damaged objects, without being able to repair them or to escape from them.

Pathological organisations

Clinically, these constellations can manifest themselves as abiding grievances, agonising self-accusations, resentment, quarrelling, chronic contriteness, utopian expectations (Weiss 2012a), being a know-it-all or feelings of moral inferiority or superiority. What is characteristic about it is that the state of suffering is maintained for a long time and any attempt to change meets with a worsening clinical condition. Frequently, stability is achieved at the cost of development while the patient tenaciously holds on to their misrepresentations of their internal and external reality.

Based on Karl Abrahams (1919; 1924) and Joan Rivière's (1936) seminal work, such states of balance were conceptualised as 'pathological organisations' (Meltzer 1968; Rosenfeld 1971; Steiner 1993), located at the borderline of the paranoid-schizoid and depressive positions where they provide protection both from persecutory guilt as well as from depressive anxieties. In 1935, Klein had already considered the introduction of a 'manic' and 'obsessional position' at the transition from the paranoid-schizoid to the depressive position. These 'positions' can be understood by their specific defence mechanisms and object relations as well as by their limited capacity for reparation under the dominance of a powerful and cruel super-ego. John Steiner (1993) expanded on these ideas coining the term 'borderline position', which describes this kind of balance between the paranoid-schizoid and the depressive position (Steiner 1987) dominated by a pathological orga-nisation. The 'borderline position' is a state marked by the offer of pseudo-stability, its resistance to change as well as by an addiction-like hold on states of psychic retreat.

In the following, I will describe such a state of retreat, which was mainly based on resentment and wrath and led to repeated impasses during the analysis. Furthermore, I would like to show how the orga-nisation, on which the retreat was founded, was based on a near-delu-sional misrepresentation of reality and brought the patient repeatedly close to suicidal crises when he was on the threshold of reparation, so that I doubted that the treatment could help him. This gave rise on my part to irritation and resignation with the consequence that my capa-city for reparation also suffered. At those moments, we got into argu-ments and I found it difficult to find my way back to an understanding stance.

Clinical vignette: wrath, resentment and the impossibility of reparation

Mr. D. is a 30-year-old employee, who grew up in a family that had moved to Germany from a completely different cultural background. His parents had emigrated from a distant country and settled at the birthplace of the patient, where his father found work. The closely connected family were scattered all over the world.

In his childhood, he was teased and ridiculed because of his foreign appearance. This, together with his parents' pressure to conform and their strict, traditional style of child education, turned his childhood into an oppressive experience of humiliation and shame. He was repeatedly beaten for minor misdemeanours and felt excluded at school as an outsider.

He tried to overcome these humiliations by doing well at school and after finishing by acquiring detailed knowledge of the international finance busi-ness. Through clever transactions on the stock market, he accrued a fortune of several million dollars by the age of 21. At the time, he was working as an employee in an insurance company. After feeling put down and wrongly criticised repeatedly by a senior colleague, he resigned from this job and decided to study economics with the aim of one day becoming a fund manager in an international trading firm, first in London and then in New York. In order to concentrate completely on his studies, he entrusted the management of his fortune to his father. However, when the father did not react quickly enough during a stock market crisis, almost the whole fortune was lost again in a short time.

The subsequent onset of depression and the constant rumination made his studies difficult for Mr. D. He could not get over the loss of his assets, brooding over his misfortune and failing his exams by a narrow margin several times. Eventually, he changed colleges and then broke off his studies altogether after an exam from his previous college was not recognised and a professor, whom he had idealised, had died. Since then, he had withdrawn from the world full of resentment and contempt. He blamed his father's 'stupidity' for his failure, refused to attempt a new beginning in life and expected instead to be given back to him what he had wrongly lost.

Thus he lived at home, tyrannising his parents, whom he accused of living in disorderly, squalid conditions, because they did not follow his 'instructions'. Related to this, as I later learned, were accusations towards the father, who had once cheated on the mother when the patient was 14 years old. He was disappointed with his mother for forgiving his father's misconduct despite the hurt it had caused her, and for staying with him.

He himself had only just once dared to voice his feelings towards a young woman and he could not cope with her rejection. In the same year, he had witnessed the terror attack on the World Trade Centre in New York. In my view, the collapse of the Twin Towers seemed to stand for the breakdown of his omnipotent self-worth as well as for the murderous rage against his parents. So he spent most of his time with financial analyses in front of his computer, self-harmed occasionally and let his parents feel his resentment. After several suicidal threats, he took up a psychoanalytic treatment (urged by his parents), which he experienced as a humiliating confirmation of his condition as well as a wasted effort to give him back his pride, success and financial independence.

Course of treatment

Mr. D. appeared desperate, but also reluctant in our first few sessions. In one way, he conveyed that he must not be left alone, but at the same time that his situation was so hopeless, that he could not be helped anyway, unless one gave back to him what had been taken from him

unjustly. His fatalistic resignation seemed touching as well as provocative. In the second assessment interview, he already mentioned that he
was not sure whether he would not plunge a knife straight into his
heart immediately after the session. I was shocked and alarmed, but
also angered about his attack and interpreted that he was putting a
knife on my chest and giving me the responsibility if things did not
work out as he wanted. He led me to understand that the treatment
was not going to change much anyway, and turned back to his angry
accusations. He cannot imagine, he said after one of the initial sessions,
that anyone had ever experienced such unjust humiliation as he had.

In subsequent sessions, his attitude towards me vacillated between
admiration, contempt and subjugation in relation to me as a cruel
figure, whose respect he longed for and who demanded 'absolute obedience' from him. As I will go on to show, this constellation included
aspects of a cruel super-ego, by which Mr. D. felt persecuted and
humiliated, but with which he was also identified in a self-righteous way.

In our sessions, Mr. D. was almost exclusively preoccupied with the
past. All my attempts to examine his current state and to lead him out of
his impasse were rejected. He regularly returned to the events which, in
his opinion, were responsible for his hopeless situation. Thus he described, for instance, in minute detail the course of the stock exchange rate in
the year 2001, the failures of his father at that time, the unjustified criticism by his superior in the insurance company in which he worked at the
time, the non-recognition of his course certificate, which seven years ago
led to him not being admitted to take his exam. While he filled the sessions in this way with monotonous accusations, I had the feeling that I
could not reach him. I often felt tired, hopeless or irritated while my futile
efforts to establish an emotional contact with him seemed to be ignored
with charitable negligence. As for Mr. D., it was clear that the treatment
came 'too late' and I was not to blame for his misery.

Many months passed in this 'tug of war': while I was trying to get him
into the present, he ignored my interpretations and pulled me back into
his past, whereby a strong sense of resentment and anger became palpable. The only 'solution', the only form of 'reparation', which he could
imagine, he said, was a restoration of the state *before* the loss of his fortune and the failure of his studies. Because he well knew that I was not in
a position to bring about this state, my interpretations were either
experienced as irrelevant or as 'needling', which left me feeling rejected
and angry. In particular, when he described his father as simple, lazy and
useless, I was more than once provoked into getting reproachful, pointing
out that he was unbearably arrogant. Although such 'rebukes', as he
called them, hurt him, he did not seem to let them get to him.

The retreat to an inaccessible island

Nevertheless, his condition stabilised after about two years and he tried to rebuild his fortune by skilful financial investments. He continued to refuse to seek regular employment, and experienced it as a 'punishment of fate', as he said, 'to have such incompetent parents as his' – an accusation from which I was ostensibly excluded, although I experienced myself, apart from some irritable confrontations, often ineffective and useless. Repeatedly, Mr. D. let me know that the 'contact with people' was disappointing and it seemed clear to me that the contact with me could only be another disappointment.

At a time when the conflicts with his parents were coming to a head, he spoke one day full of contempt about not wanting to have 'anything more to do with this world'.

Then he sketched out the picture of a desolate island to which he had retreated and had put up a big sign 'No trespassing' for all who passed by. From this island, he was going to follow the world-wide stock exchanges in the hope of regaining his previous wealth by clever investment and thus lead a life of independence and affluence. While others were prohibited from getting close to the island, I was allowed from time to time to come ashore in a small boat in order to deliver food supplies. But, he said, even I was not permitted access to the 'darker areas' inside the island.

To me this picture seemed as much imaginative as provocative. While I attempted to interpret his isolation and his self-righteous wrath, Mr. D. let me know that I did indeed not have access to these 'darker areas' inside of him. Thus a helplessness spread inside me, which went so far that I found myself one day beginning to carefully check the stock exchange rates in the absurd hope that if they rose, the patient would get better...

It seemed that I had lost all confidence in my work and instead had become identified with his omnipotent belief system. I thought, the 'provisions' I was allowed to deliver were merely serving to preserve the status quo, to nourish his resentment and his superiority, without finding real access to his internal world.

Emerging from the retreat and moving back into it

Nevertheless, there were times when a better contact developed between us. When, after one of my interpretations, he wanted to start with the sentence: 'In the year 2000...' (and I expected the usual complaints about his father's failures, the unfair treatment by his superior, the discrimination by his academic teachers), he continued by saying:

Figure 3 Ursula Haug (London), Bamburgh Castle, Oil on canvas, 2005
(Private collection; photographic adaptation: © Carina Weiss)

'In the year 2000, I would not have understood your interpretations'. To my surprise, he added that, if he understood me correctly, his all-or-nothing attitude was the greatest problem and thus he was his worst enemy. After a short pause, he let me know that he had been invited to friends in Switzerland who organised white-water rafting tours for tourists together with expert guides from New Zealand.

I had the impression that telling me about this invitation expressed an appetite for life. This raised my hopes and I said that maybe he was considering trusting my guidance in moving off his desperate island into rough waters.

However, he responded that someone who has never had the experience of failure like me would never be likely to understand him, and I immediately had the feeling that I was given another lecture on failure and misunderstanding.

But it was difficult for Mr. D. to feel understood by me, because, from his point of view, I was in an ideal position, furnished with all the attributes he longed for: money, prestige, academic title and a family.

This engendered such envy in him that while he found my 'analysis correct', he insisted that I could never put myself in his position.

Thus Mr. D. could 'understand' my interpretations on an intellectual level, but for a long time could not really take them in or make use of them, because his problem was his lacking capacity for reparation. Instead of acknowledging the damage he inflicted on others, he was constantly preoccupied with the injustice done to him. Thus, he projected his wish for reparation and *demanded reparation from others*, who should return to him what he had been unfairly denied, particularly money, success and respect for his person. For this reason, reparation meant to him *concrete restitution* rather than making amends.

Thus, Mr. D. experienced life and the analysis as a constant humiliation. He despised dependency and longed to re-establish an illusory state, where everything belonged to him and he was not dependent on anyone. From his solitary island, he *tolerated* the analysis as long as it provided him with food for his illusions and his campaign for revenge. However, he seemed to reject it whenever it demanded change in him and confronted *him* with being in touch with the reality of mourning and loss.

Wrath – the impossibility of reparation

In this hopeless situation, time passed by without any prospect of change. It became increasingly clear that Mr. D. was in the grip of a cruel super-ego, which either offered him moral superiority or enforced absolute obedience. He claimed the higher moral values for himself and thus justified his withdrawal from other people, though he regretted not having been able to have a relationship with a woman.

Feelings of humiliation could easily and quickly turn into states of rage and indignation, from where he looked down on other people. Then he complained in endless litanies about the 'stupidity' of his parents and their numerous shortcomings. He could spend whole sessions in contemptuous outpourings that his mother had used a metal fork in a non-stick frying pan despite his repeated 'warnings', and his father, who had no table manners, drove like an idiot, wouldn't put in his hearing aids and generally did not follow his well-meant advice and 'instructions', which is why he stopped talking to him. During this tirade his voice got louder and louder and he worked himself into a state of excited rage. He described his parents as 'hopeless cases' and wondered how much longer he would be 'patient' with them.

In turn, I increasingly experienced *him* as my hopeless case and frequently felt at the end of my tether. When I attempted to interpret his accusations as being directed against me, he usually indulgently ignored this. However, when he experienced my interventions as critical, he either knuckled under obediently or stopped talking to me, and at times this led to loud confrontations during which I got carried away into reproaching him, something I had meant to really avoid. At such moments, I asked myself what my colleague working next door would think when she overheard these exchanges from her room.

In the case of the scratched non-stick Teflon pan, he had accused his mother of 'poisoning' the food, while I countered that he did not want to see that he was poisoning other people's food with his angry accusations.

There followed a long silence, before he returned to the next session reproachful and hurt, talking again about his mother's misdemeanours. Now I interpreted that he had experienced my comment just like the sharp fork of his mother, destroying the thin protective layer inside of him and poisoning his nourishment.

He seemed to experience this interpretation as absurd, but appeared to listen carefully. In a livelier and more direct way, he protested against my view of his moral superiority by saying he had a right to think like that. But then his protest flipped into indignation and he declared:

> Because of my setbacks and unjust humiliations, I have developed a strict moral code. And if you think that I live from a position of moral superiority or you even think that a 'laissez-faire' attitude towards my parents would be a better solution, then I am definitely of a different opinion.

This indignation could rapidly turn into wrath and then his contempt and hatred assumed self-destructive dimensions. As he got more worked up in his anger, his accusations got louder and sharper and in equal measure the damage he inflicted on himself and his objects increased. The chance of reconciliation and understanding was then far removed, because in angry indignation, reparation can only be thought of as *mercy* and it is exactly that what makes the idea of reconciliation so unthinkable. I felt reminded of Milton's *Paradise Lost* and thought that my patient obviously thought 'Better to reign in Hell, then serve in Heaven' (Milton 1667, Book 1, 263).

Thus the therapy had to be conducted in this 'hell', and why should I be spared from going through hell with him? It seemed that I was either identified with his contemptible parents or with his vengeful super-ego, which believed itself to be in possession of superior moral standards in my omnipotent belief that I could change him. Evidently, I had to concede the failure of my own expectations, before I could take in some of his helplessness and distress. In any case, after his self-righteous moral declaration he felt very alone and let me know after a long weekend that he felt worse without the sessions. On this occasion, a more desperate sadness and affection came to the fore, which had previously been absent.

On the threshold of the depressive position – despair and retreat

The conflict with his parents, however, escalated when they accepted a wedding invitation abroad. He had refused to accompany them and felt contempt for his parents who had accepted the relatives' offer to pay for the travel costs. In 'absolute obedience', he drove the parents to the airport, but did not talk to them nor look at them when saying good-bye. At home, he unplugged the phone so that he would be out of reach for them. They should be left in the lurch, not knowing how he was, should be plagued by guilt during the wedding festivities while suicidal phantasies and the projection of responsibility and guilt dominated his ideation.

This situation was mirrored in the treatment, when he said that he would 'not advise anyone' to get in contact with him. He added that he was on 'the path of self-destruction' saying that 'the coldness inside' of him was coming to a head and that he could do to himself what others had done to him.

I interpreted, that here too he had taken the plug out sending me warning signals and letting me know that nobody could prevent him from harming himself.

He reacted with an angry outburst of rage, saying he was pleased that his parents were finally away, asserting that only he could help himself by rebuilding his fortune. Otherwise, life was meaningless for him.

I suggested that he regarded my efforts as pretty useless, felt desperately alone and doubted that anyone could take in his despair. As I said this, I had little hope of being able to reach him and felt that I was close to giving up.

It was at moments like this that the mood in the sessions changed and Mr. D. got into a state of deep sadness. Then his superiority and rage collapsed and he seemed desperate and helpless. The possibility of suicide was no longer the mighty threat in the room, but a last resort at the edge of his despair. I feared that it would be just at such a time when he let go of the predominance of his destructive internal organisation that he could do something to himself and said to him that he attempted to hold himself together with his resentment, superiority and wrath, so as not to be overwhelmed by sadness, dependency and guilt. He replied that he agreed with my analysis, *but he just could not forgive.*

Much to my surprise, he told me in the last session before the Christmas break that he had replied to Christmas cards for the first time in years and was planning to visit friends abroad. After he had said his goodbyes, he turned around once more with tears in his eyes, saying: 'And thank you for always being here for me in the past year'.

Such moments could be very touching and gave a glimpse of a capacity for gratitude, which had been hidden for a long time. Mr. D. worried that he might not be able to finance the four-times-weekly sessions once the health insurance stopped paying, although I had indicated that I was prepared to make financial accommodations for him. He wanted to know whether he would be allowed to return to the analysis at a later date and whether I was prepared to have him back, and he announced that if he were to make money on the stock exchange, he would invest it in his analysis. His mother had said to him that he should not worry too much about his future and he had begun to talk more with his father again.

These movements made me feel hopeful, but could easily be obscured when humiliation and shame became too strong. At such times, his accusations and wrath grew to monstrous proportions and he withdrew once again into his defensive system, when he 'ordered about' his parents like disobedient children, wishing them dead and talking to me about his three 'fundamental premises' that were the basis for any possible change, namely: regaining his lost fortune, that others carried the guilt and therefore had to change first and thirdly, that time had to reverse and the bad experiences of his childhood had to be undone.

Conclusions

Mr. D.'s three anti-therapeutic 'fundamental premises' illustrate the basis of his defensive system and his near-delusional misrepresentation of reality. He felt debased by his professional failure and the humiliating experiences of his childhood and demanded that others took responsibility for this. Because of the tenacity with which he held on to his resentment and the omnipotence of his wrath, any effort at reparation seemed near enough impossible for a long time. His way of dealing with his primitive super-ego was to identify with its ideal, omnipotent aspects as well as with its cruel, persecutory ones, so that he felt superior to his parents and entitled to look down on them and to humiliate them.

In this context, Roger Money-Kyrle (1962) spoke about an envious usurpation of the super-ego by the ego. Through this take-over, the ego assumes megalomaniac traits and liberates itself from the dependency on its conscience. Persecutory guilt is left behind and turns itself into 'an envious assertion of moral superiority without any morals' (Bion 1962, p. 97). Therefore Bion talks about 'a super-ego that has hardly any of the characteristics of the super-ego as understood in psychoanalysis: it is a "super" ego' (ibid.). However, this denuding of guilt comes at a high price, in particular, loneliness and being cut off from human contact and psychic development, as it was clearly expressed in Mr. D.'s idea of his dominion on his desolate island, where nobody was allowed to alight.

In the analysis, both sides of his super-ego were projected into me, so that I appeared either as an ideal object to him who constantly evoked his envy, or as a cruel object who demanded 'absolute obedience', humiliated him and constantly criticised him with 'sharp rebukes'.

For a long time, there seemed to be no way out of this situation and I had to resist the temptation of putting the blame on *him* for my own failure and lack of success and demanding that *he* should change. In doing so, I was unconsciously identified with Mr. D. as someone who knew no other way of dealing with failure and disappointment than projecting their guilt into others. Thus we got into a situation in which each one of us demanded from the other to change, an impasse in which resentment and revenge can flourish, but reparation is very difficult.

As I mentioned earlier, in her 1958 paper, Melanie Klein pointed out that the ego and the super-ego *can only change together*. In this she stresses a different priority to Ronald Britton, who in his paper 'Emancipation from the super-ego' (Britton 2003), put forward the notion of a release of the ego from the domination of the archaic super-ego. According to Klein, however, changes in the ego and super-ego are only possible concurrently. This means that changes in the ego function presuppose that the super-ego loses some of its omnipotence and cruelty. Only then on the threshold to the depressive position can feelings of guilt become more bearable and a process of reparation can begin. To quote Klein: 'At this stage the injured object is no longer predominantly felt as a persecutor, but as a loved object towards whom a feeling of guilt and the urge to make reparation are experienced' (Klein, 1958, pp. 241–242).

What Klein is describing here is the transformation of the super-ego from a pathological organisation into a helpful instance, which assists the ego in dealing with its worst anxieties while still setting boundaries, and is concerned about the 'maintenance' or even the 'retrieval' of the lost 'good object' (see Brenman 2006). In this situation, the super-ego no longer wreaks punishment and revenge but is brought to act in the service of reconciliation and reparation:

SE ↔ R

In turn, the trust in the possibility of reparation strengthens the capacity for mourning and for overcoming resentment, thus overcoming the repetition compulsion, and turning towards life.

In Mr. D., such efforts at reparation were initially only noticeable for brief moments, when his mood became sadder and I, too, felt helpless, not knowing how to proceed further. Nevertheless, these movements were never entirely absent and at times made him feel so desperate that it was not just him, but me who feared that any progress in the analysis could lead to him actually harming himself, as if he could only survive as long as he held on to his resentment and wrath. I think it was in these moments that Mr. D. was close to the threshold of the depressive position.

As soon as the emerging anxiety and feelings of guilt became unbearable, however, he once again withdrew into the protection of his defensive organisation. Similarly to Mr. A. and Mr. C., described in the previous chapter, he then appeared almost unreachable and retreated. Like Mr. A., he blamed the unfair treatment by others for his miserable state.

As often in such constellations, the idea of a 'non-partisan' third party who observes and explores the circumstances seems very difficult, and such a position is not conceded to the analyst either. He is rather expected to be on the side of the patient, supporting him in his struggle against the figures who have hurt him, or else to become such a figure himself continuing to humiliate him and even blaming him for the condition he is in. With the example of Mr. A., I have tried to show how rapidly such a switch can happen and the analyst becomes the guilty one from whom remorse is expected. In this way, resentment can be described as a state in which the wounds are kept open and *the wish for reparation is projected into an object to whom any possibility of reparation is denied.* Thus, the object will be plagued by endless feelings of guilt.

During treatment, the analyst can make the experience of how difficult it is to heal wounds, which have to be kept open for internal motives and to enable reparation where reparation is not permitted – a Sisyphus task, which confronts him again and again with his failure and with the function of the repetition compulsion. In this way, the patient comes to stand for the *analyst's own damaged inner objects.* Nevertheless, I believe that this constellation is analysable as long as the analyst does not proceed in the same way, namely projecting his/her damaged internal objects into the patient. It is only in this case that a symmetrical impasse develops by unconsciously demanding the patient to improve in order to repair the analyst's own internal state.

In my view, this dynamic is characteristic of the structure of resentment where *gaze* is often used as a means for projection. In resentment, the gaze is directed in an accusatory way from below to above, while in wrath it goes contemptuously from above to below. Unlike Mr. C., who degraded himself in self-accusations, Mr. D. did not experience guilt for a long time. In his anger, he seemed rather identified with a morally superior position, in which he deemed himself to be god-like and the world too bad for deserving his love. In such a position, reparation can only take the form of mercy.

Both states of mind, grievance and wrath, rendered the processing of guilt very difficult for a long time. Instead of enabling reparation, they evoked further humiliation and contrition, which in turn nourished the need for revenge and thus perpetuated the repetition compulsion and the damage to the internal objects. Mr. D. was well able to see this vicious cycle for some time and even agreed with my 'analyses', as he put it, but he just could not *forgive*.

I believe, though, that *genuine understanding* is bound up with the possibility of reparation. While humiliation and shame require immediate relief, reparation takes time; time to acknowledge the damage which one has done to others, the recognition that certain developments cannot be reversed and therefore the need to acknowledge transience and loss. And it is exactly this painful experience, the acknowledgement of mourning and loss, which is the pre-condition for reparation. Alfred Schöpf (2005 p. 111) put it this way: 'only when this pain is felt (…) and lived, feelings of reconciliation and reparation can sally forth and only then a way out of violence can be found'. It is exactly this painful step which Mr. D. tried to avoid by withdrawing into a timeless state of mind. The sole possibility of reparation according to the third of his 'fundamental premises' was a *reversal of time,* meaning the illusion of a return to paradise.

Maybe this does not just apply to the individual mind, but also to certain social developments, where the repetition compulsion takes over when reparation fails. Looked at in this way, Mr. D.'s third premise corresponds with a backward-looking, historic utopia (see Weiss 2012a).

The significance of *timelessness* in states of psychic retreat will be dealt with in the following chapters. In contrast to the standstill of time, reparation brings about the imponderability and irreversibility of time, but also the pain that is connected to it. This means that hurt associated with severe trauma cannot be reversed, but must not dominate experience forever.

Concerning the question what makes such reparative movements possible, I would like to refer to Roger Money-Kyrle's (1956) early paper on counter-transference, where he says that by projecting his internal objects into the analyst the patient comes to stand for the analyst's own damaged internal objects. In his view, true understanding goes along with the *analyst's* capacity for reparation. In Mr. D's analysis, I had reached a point more than once where I felt hopeless in the face of his mighty, angry accusations and had lost all hope for development and change. Then I projected my helplessness and impotence back into him and held him responsible for my failure.

It was only in those moments when I had to acknowledge my limits to help and to understand and was close to giving up, that Mr. D. too could acknowledge his loneliness and despair. It seemed, as John Steiner put it in a recent paper (Steiner 2011c), as if both analyst and patient had to experience the collapse of their omnipotence to recognise the limits of what is achievable and devise realistic goals.

In the case of Mr. D. this meant, as he once put it, that the 'surf' of the 'breaking waves' against his lonely island was getting smaller and he could ask me whether he might be able to return. I think with this question he expressed his insecurity about whether I would be able to forgive him. In his paper on reparation, Henry Rey (1986) suggested that the development of a capacity to forgive is in turn linked to the possibility of being able to imagine *to be forgiven*. In this way, I think, Mr. D.'s problems were not resolved by analysis, but maybe it helped him to live with them.

How can the acknowledgement of damages, the overcoming of the repetition compulsion and a new appreciation of life take shape in psychoanalytic treatment? How do analyst and patient find their way out of the entanglements into which they are drawn by the pull of traumatic experiences? And what are the steps by which the movements towards reparation gradually gain strength and stability in the face of the pervasive tendency of repetition? These questions are the concern of the following two chapters in the context of Mrs. E.'s analysis.

Chapter 4

The 'Tower'

Submission and illusory security in a traumatic defence organisation

Pathological organisations of the personality such as Mr. D's based on resentment and revenge present themselves in different ways. They can be expressed in dreams and complex fantasy systems or enacted in interpersonal relationships with the consequence that others become involved or even become part of these systems. This is the basis of various forms of enmeshment and re-enactment, but it also provides a prospect for change. During the course of a psychoanalytic treatment, one can gain a closer understanding of the structure and function of such organisations. Often, they are represented in the patient's dream material, fantasies and memories or are actually mirrored in the transference situation.

Mr. D's 'desolate island' provides such an example. It describes a retreat from where he could observe the ups and downs of the world, allowing for limited contact with other people, but ultimately everything is kept under control. The solitariness and sadness of his position are hidden behind an illusory mantle of power, control and invulnerability as well as mistrust of anyone who comes close. This applies for the analyst as well, who is allowed from time to time to disembark in order to provide food, but is not permitted access to the darker areas of his island.

Places of psychic retreat are *spatial representations* of pathological organisations of the personality (Steiner 1993). Occasionally, they are conceptualised as a safe haven or, as in the classic utopian imagination, as paradise islands beyond the experience of time (Morus 1516; Hall 1605; Campanella 1623; Bacon 1627; Andreae 1619; see Weiss 2012a; Eco 2013). At other times, theses retreats are represented as caves or hiding places, which provide protection from cold, threat and pain or, as in the case of Mr. D, provide an 'exclusion zone'. Sometimes, they are represented by the affiliation with an exclusive group, association or sect or the identification with overvalued ideas beyond doubt and contact with reality. In a recent paper, Esther Horn (2015) described the structure and function of such an 'inner sect organisation', whose main task was to transform anxiety about violence and guilt into an erotised, masochistic retreat. What all these states have in common is that they initially provide a refuge, which gradually turns into a prison and eventually into a dungeon without a way of escape (see Steiner 1993; Weiss 2009).

In these labyrinths, any development gets stuck, but at the same time their timelessness seems to protect from persecution and threatening change. In the analysis, such patients appear sometimes unreachable (Joseph 1975) and not infrequently, the treatment itself is transformed into a place of psychic retreat. In such a case, a paradoxical situation arises in which the therapy seems to maintain the state it sets out to change.

In my view, this dilemma is more or less unavoidable in patients with highly complex psychic retreats. Analyst and analysand have then to live through these dead ends before a realistic picture of the possibilities and limits of psychic change can emerge. Only then, a loophole out of the seemingly intractable situation can open up and step by step enable the patient to relinquish their psychic retreat (see Steiner 2014).

The female patient I am going to present had retreated into the structure of a 'tower', which served as a refuge for her fantasies. In this tower, she was tormented by anonymous men, who eventually got her into a state of 'belonging', as she put it, making her feel close to her tormentors and absolutely secure under their protection. This fantasy frequently made her lapse into daydreams and at night time, particularly when on her own, it gave her solace and helped her go to sleep.

In the analysis, it took about half a year before she could tell me about these ideas. She was worried that, by communicating them, these ideas would lose their power and that the 'men in the tower', whom she referred to as 'her friends', would withhold their protection.

In this way, the analysis was seen as a threat to the security which she experienced in her dungeon. But at the same time, it was experienced as ineffective, as I was the only person who knew about her torment, which I was just helplessly witnessing, but could not change. It emerged that the idea of a person who *'knows everything'* that is going on in the tower, but is unable to intervene, formed an important part of her fantasy.

I would like to go on to show the pervasive influence this pathological organisation, represented by the 'tower', had on the patient's life and how threatened she felt by the possibility of moving out of her dungeon. When, after one and a half years of treatment, she attempted steps in this direction, she dreaded that the move would be irreversible and she repeatedly feared that she was going to go mad. In one of these situations, she said: *'I hope you know what you are doing!'*

The subsequent shifts in the analysis can be roughly summarised in four phases:

Figure 4 Maschikuli-Tower, Fortress Marienberg, Würzburg (© Carina Weiss)

- In a *first phase*, she found herself absolutely loyal to her oppressors as well as to me.
- In the *second phase*, she got into an irresolvable conflict of loyalty.
- In the *third phase*, she moved out of the dominance of her pathological organisation, but was then threatened by chaos and confusion and feeling dependent on me, like a puppet on a string.
- Finally, in a *fourth phase*, she felt decidedly better having reached a kind of 'coexistence' between her now weakened pathological organisations and her analysis.

Representing the treatment in 'phases' like this is, of course, a simplification of complex, intertwined processes, which were at times parallel, at times mixed up, moving back and forth, on occasion creating insecurity and confusion in me. Nevertheless, I thought that, in the first three years of Mrs. E's analysis, there were developments, which led to noticeable changes. It was initially unclear whether further development was going to be possible. Towards the end of this chapter, I will indicate in which direction these changes were going. In the subsequent chapter, I will deal with the significance of reparative processes which gradually emerged.

Clinical material

The 27-year-old patient, kind, frequently shy with a seemingly childlike helplessness alternating with an elegant, 'correct' and ladylike demeanour, got herself into analysis two years after her father's premature death and a few months after she had got married herself. She had cared for her father prior to his death and had organised his funeral without allowing herself any feelings of grief and mourning, which she considered to be impermissible and unforgivable signs of 'weakness'. She was actually *convinced that she was fundamentally bad* and saw the sole justification of her existence in *surviving to function for others*; for only by being there 'unconditionally' for others, she believed, could she compensate for her faultiness and guilt to some degree.

As I would like to show, the conviction of her badness paradoxically formed the basis of some feeling of security. For as long as she could feel bad and worthless, she at least knew *who she was*. As soon as she experienced anything good, however, she reacted with confusion and feelings of guilt.

In this way, Mrs. E. got into a bad state soon after she had married her husband who evidently loved her. She lost weight, re-started self-harming as she had done in her childhood, and was absorbed in thoughts of accidents, incurable diseases and the belief that her husband would soon leave her. As she said, these thoughts, together with the torments in the 'tower', provided some 'relief' for her.

Biography

In the course of the analysis, Mrs. E.'s atrocious life history was gradually revealed to me. She was the elder of two siblings who grew up in a desolate situation with a largely absent or drunk mother, and a father who, overwhelmed by depressive feelings, denied the domestic misery and occasionally lost control in his helplessness.

The mother was suspected of having been party to the violent death of her first husband. During the patient's childhood, she was repeatedly detained for countless crimes of fraud, while the family sank into poverty as the debts could not be settled. At times, she and her sister were left alone in the flat for days without food until mother reappeared in a chaotic state, drunk and screaming. Often, she was in an uncontrollable mood shifting between exaltation, confusion and helpless despair and, in this state, she was unreachable. Repeatedly she had uttered that her life had been ruined through the patient's birth. The children were neglected and, as early as age two, Mrs. E. was admitted to hospital due to dehydration. The same happened when the patient was 11 years old: she refused to eat and wanted to die. She said she had hoped that in this way she would relieve her mother from the burden of her existence.

Much later, I learned that the mother had not only prostituted herself, but 'lent' the patient to a circle of paedophile men over a long period of time. It seems that this abuse eventually produced 'the men in the tower' who in her fantasy were turned from persecutors into protectors. In her imagination, they threatened her if she would 'talk' about them. Although it was no longer a death threat, she would lose their protection and be exposed to chaos and confusion.

Based on this, a pathological organisation had emerged, shielding her from confusion and fears of fragmentation. The promise of the organisation was to turn persecution into security by establishing an identification with cruel, powerful objects, on the understanding that the patient would in turn comply with its principles and relinquish her own life. At the same time, the dungeon in the tower represented a powerful super-ego, offering 'order' and freedom from feelings of guilt at the cost of suffering. At a later stage, the patient described that this 'life in hell' had for a long time been the only possibility of survival and she frequently wished herself back there.

When she was 15, her parents got divorced. By this time, she had long taken over the running of the household, looking after her younger sister and her father who met another woman. Despite all these pressures, she was able to finish her school education and find employment as an officer with a large security firm. Everything in this company, down to the smallest detail, was regulated by rules, procedures and instructions, which met her needs for subordination and discipline. She met her first boyfriend, who showed her up and humiliated her for years before she managed to separate from him and met her future husband. She attempted to 'erase' the relationship with her mother, who was not to know where she lived, whether or not she had got married or what name she now had. At the same time, she was convinced that she would end up like her mother, sink into chaos, overwhelmed by greed and cruelty, and indeed she felt she was already exactly like her. For this reason, she banned herself from thinking about having her own children.

Before the patient came to analysis, she had been living in a state of 'sedation' for years, having been treated more or less unsuccessfully with neuroleptics, antidepressants, tranquilisers and behaviour therapy. Her self-harming had started in childhood and went hand in hand with eating disorders, stomach and intestinal problems, excruciating inner turmoil and the ongoing constant wish to be able to die soon. It emerged later that the stomach and intestinal cramps had started following a dream in which she was supposed to eat a snake sandwich. This 'snake', possibly a combination of a sadistic penis and a poisonous breast, seemed to bite and torture her from inside and led to never-ending endoscopic investigations.

The fact that her husband loved her and she had been able to have an initially satisfying emotional and sexual relationship with him seemed to confuse her. From her point of view, she did not 'deserve' this. This state of affairs seemed to her as unreal as the fact that the analysis was about to understand her inner despair. She did hope that the treatment would improve her condition, but in the sense that she could 'function' again and become the way I had in mind for her.

Course of treatment

This may explain why we had completely different ideas about her treatment from the very beginning. While I was trying to provide her with a space to make unbearable feelings more bearable (Riesenberg-Malcolm & Roth 1999), she missed clear rules and 'instructions' from me. Thus, she tried to 'read between the lines', attempting to infer my expectations of her from what I said. For instance, for her it was clear that she had to get 'healthy' in order to 'function' at work and to reward me in my therapeutic efforts. Furthermore, she assumed that she had to be absolutely punctual, not a minute too early or too late; she was not to lean against the back of the chair while waiting, because she could quickly be 'thrown out' if she did not meet my demands. I found it hard to adopt this role of a cruel, authoritarian figure and I realised that I repeatedly tried to avoid this by striving to be particularly sympathetic and understanding.

Mrs. E. seemed to be touched by this, but at the same time it confused her. She experienced my attitude towards her as unreal and at times feared that it was a 'trap' to make her dependent on me in order to drop her. At the same time, she took her sessions very seriously and was deeply saddened by occasional cancellations; so much so that I was touched by her sadness and at times dazed and confused by the devotion and trust she invested in me.

Subservience

What I had lost sight of in all of this, however, was that this devotion was largely based on subservience. There were indeed many sessions in which the patient appeared with almost military discipline, elegant and correctly dressed; then I could hear her staccato steps in the corridor. In greeting me, she lowered her gaze, lay on the couch and began dutifully to report what she thought I wanted to hear. She seemed keen to meet my expectations. Discipline and subservience were of utmost importance to her. In such sessions, she appeared to be cool, business-like and distanced, but this flipped easily into desperate helplessness and sadness. These moments, particularly when she was unable to suppress her tears, were 'unforgiveable' in her view. She experienced such moments as 'moaning' and was convinced that I would not forgive such 'weakness' in her.

For a long time, Mrs. E. found it problematic that I did not openly declare my expectations of her. She was convinced that I had a plan which she had to fulfil. In her view, I followed a particularly cruel strategy by leaving her in the dark about my objectives. This way she could only 'get it wrong' while being completely at my mercy. When I talked to her about her sadness and her anxiety of being dependent on me leaving her to guess as to what my actual plans were, she was touched, but predominantly confused. She thought that personal feelings were not allowed in therapy and I would treat her 'professionally', meaning without feelings, although her dependency and vulnerability were very palpable in the room.

She told me her life history, about her devastating childhood, about her cold murderous hatred of her mother, about the men who abused her, as if I were a 'neutral' person who needed this information to arrive at therapeutic conclusions about her. She assumed that I would not use the material she entrusted me with against her, although the similarities between the analytic situation and the 'strange men' she had been handed over to could not be overlooked. When I took up this topic at one time, talking about her disquiet and feelings of unreality caused by a room-change due to building work in the clinic, she spontaneously replied: 'I had no idea what to expect behind this door'.

I frequently felt that there was a terrible misunderstanding growing between us. While I was trying to create more space and understanding for her soft, affectionate and vulnerable sides, she believed that I was contemptuous of her and regarded these features as a 'lack of discipline'. To criticise me was totally 'forbidden' and actually quite unthinkable, because safety was only achievable through complete agreement and total compliance. In this way, she mentioned on one occasion, she had managed to hear my interpretations as 'orders'.

I was quite shocked when she told me this. But she went on to explain that in her company's manual, an 'order' was defined by the following *three elements:*

- firstly, analysis of the situation,
- secondly, exploration of possible courses of action and
- thirdly, determination and control of execution.

I had to concede that my interpretations did indeed contain parts of these elements, but took solace in the thought that the security company she worked for was probably less pathologically structured than her cruel super-ego organisation, which so dominated and terrorised her internally. Therefore, I began to think that my interpretations/ 'orders' might possibly help her weather her internal catastrophes.

The conflict between the analysis and the pathological organisation

However, my belief was most likely naïve in that I continued to hope that I was not going to become part of the cruel organisation which dominated Mrs. E. internally. When she told me for the first time about her daydreams of 'the men in the tower', she was very anxious. As I have already mentioned, linked in with this fantasy was the idea of a person outside the tower, who 'knows everything' but is condemned to be a helpless witness.

I interpreted that the analysis was most likely represented by this third powerless person outside the tower and she became immediately alarmed and experienced acute feelings of guilt.

I responded by saying that she seemed to feel guilty because she heard my comment as a harsh criticism, as if she had made me into a weak, helpless figure, who had to witness everything without being able to intervene and therefore I was going to be reproachful. I added that she feared I would punish her for that or even 'throw her out', as she had voiced repeatedly.

Mrs. E. now found herself in a precarious situation fearing that she might lose everything: on the one hand, the sessions and her hope of change; on the other hand, 'the men in the tower', who would never forgive her disloyalty and who would punish her even harder or withdraw their protection. Indeed, one of her greatest anxieties was that the fantasy, once voiced, was going to lose its power and she would no longer be able to calm herself with the images of torment and suffering.

These imaginations contained all sorts of cruelties such as rape, serious skin damages as well as disfigurement and crippling fractures. They were, however, only weakly erotised but contained the central idea of 'survival by discipline', that is the idea that if she did not resist or struggle, but bore the cruelties, she was going to be accepted into the circle of her 'friends' and would be protected from all suffering in life.

By divulging this secret to me, she got into a conflict of loyalty with her inner organisation. Indeed, this fantasy, which had been at her disposal until then, began to lose its calming effect and in her imagination, she felt at times humiliated and insulted after the sessions.

An internal voice, identified by her as a 'policeman', shouted at her and mocked her, accusing her of being base and worthless. The voice said that she had just used the session to 'moan' once again. She would be thought of as even worse than before. She could not raise her gaze until she had left the hospital. Because now everybody knew... The way to the car park was sheer public humiliation. When she reached the car, the voice said that she could sit up again and straighten her shoulders. She should put on her 'uniform' and go to work. And she obeyed, went to work and 'functioned'.

This was the session in which she had told me about the torments of her childhood. Feelings of guilt arose in her when I suggested that the 'friends in the tower' originated from a gradual transformation of those men who had abused her in childhood. If this were the case, she said, she too was guilty and 'complicit'.

This reaction gives a flavour of the difficulty in saying anything that would not raise feelings of guilt in the patient. Nevertheless, the idea that she had become 'complicit' over time contained an important insight also.

Clinical material from a subsequent session

She began the next session with the admission that she had prepared internally for this session and felt guilty for 'controlling' me in this way. She imagined that I demanded that she talked more about the abuse in her childhood, that this was the only topic and focus of her therapy, and actually the only thing of interest about her. If she could not meet my demand, I would regard this as 'sabotaging' her analysis.

I responded by saying that she evidently feared being abused by me. I might develop a prying interest in her worst experiences and thus expose her to shame and humiliation all over again.

She was shocked by my comment. This would imply that abuse could even happen here. Then she went silent for a while and seemed very sad. She tried in vain to fight her tears and said that she had to fill her head with 'cotton wool' after the session to get rid of her feelings.

After a further silence, she added that she had occasionally tried to hint at her horrible experiences but it had always gone wrong. Her former boyfriend had humiliated her further. Her husband was at a loss how to react, which she interpreted as indifference, and most recently when he brought up the topic, she felt utter despair.

I said that she seemed to have devised a script for today's session as she obviously feared that something might go awry here. I would further humiliate her by wanting to 'know everything', or, like her husband, I would feel helpless or indifferent. Or else such sadness and despair would overwhelm her so that she would have to fill her head with 'cotton wool'.

She cried, saying that she thought of her mother with sadness for the first time. What had been wrong with her? How could she have done this to her children? These thoughts were too confusing for her. Up until now she could only think of her full of hatred or 'disciplined indifference'. But now she was completely confused...

The confusion and helplessness were clearly palpable when she said good-bye and left the room.

Discussion

Such sessions marked progress despite the considerable difficulties we were facing. They demonstrated that the patient instantly erected a new 'tower' in the session by inviting me to humiliate her further and to develop a voyeuristic interest in her worst experiences. If she could not engage me in this way, I could be in the role of the onlooker who sees everything and suffers alongside her without being able to interfere. But even that was a pretty unbearable position and at times I felt the emergence of rescue fantasies in me, when I had the feeling that I was the only good figure in her life, who could take her out of her sadistic organisation and liberate her. It should have been clear to me that the evocation of such fantasies was just another variation of keeping the status quo and maintain control.

However, there were moments – and I hope the clinical material will convey an impression of this – when the patient lost control and appeared touchingly helpless and affectionate. At such moments, when she temporarily relinquished her compliance and iron discipline, her 'protective armour' as she called it, she became overwhelmed by sadness.

At the beginning of treatment, such movements were limited and could rapidly flip into renewed humiliation and denigration. The organisation regarded such movements with utter mistrust, taunting and ridiculing her. This repeatedly triggered states of withdrawal and negative therapeutic reactions, and made sure that her sadness was rapidly turned into confusion, chaos and a sense of unreality.

Chaos and confusion

One reason for this, as already mentioned, was that for Mrs. E. only *bad experiences* were *real experiences*. The underlying belief system went back to her childhood and seemed to structure her entire experience of reality.

She herself once remarked that *only the bad can be real*, which conversely implied that *reality was bad and the good was unreal*. Consequently, in as much as the analysis contained hope for change, it belonged to the category of good, but 'unreal' experiences.

Furthermore, Mrs. E. was convinced that *only her badness could give her a sense of identity*, while finding anything good inside her triggered confusion, paranoia and unbearable feelings of guilt, because she did not deserve anything good. Either she did not deserve it, or it was a misleading illusion.

This kind of splitting posed a considerable problem in our work. It meant that whenever there was something good to be taken in, she got into a state of 'dissolution'. In that way, the analysis was a constant threat to her sense of identity. On the other hand, she gave me the impression that she was desperately dependent on the therapy, that she needed our sessions to store something good and protect it from envious internal objects and from inner destructiveness.

In the second year of analysis, these destructive forces manifested themselves when her 'old order', represented by the iron discipline and the 'men in the tower', was challenged by a series of painful changes in her life, and did no longer function reliably.

To begin with, her paternal grandmother became seriously ill and subsequently died. She had possibly been the only 'good' figure in her childhood. Mrs. E. looked after her and needed cancel occasional sessions to drive to the grandmother, who lived a long distance away. She had actually hoped that she could organise this loss and the funeral in the same way as she had done it in the past with her father's illness and death. But now, feelings of mourning and loss came up in her reminding her of her father and she had no way to dim these.

In addition, her fears that her husband might be leading a 'double life' were born out, which confirmed her view of the marriage – and of her analysis – as one of those 'good' but 'unreal' experiences. Her husband had consumed much more alcohol than he had previously admitted, he had lost money while gambling and had sought contact with other women over the internet. She found all this out when he collapsed at home in a drunken state, splintering the glass table on which he fell as well as her illusions. She took him to hospital and tried to talk to him. A lot of what was happening reminded her of her mother. What was worst for her, however, was that she felt dependent on him, but could no longer believe his protestation that he loved her. She wanted him to be 'honest' with her, but had no idea how things would continue.

Everything seemed to falter in this situation. She lost weight, developed stomach and intestinal troubles, failed to go to work for several weeks and missed occasional sessions. When I attempted to interpret her withdrawal and her return to unbearable feelings in our sessions, she experienced this as a serious accusation that I was so disappointed by her that I would no longer want to see her.

In her perception, everything seemed to get drowned out. In the sessions, she appeared as if 'sedated', evidently confused and not really there. She was most perturbed that 'the men in the tower' were no longer at her disposal. She said that the analysis had robbed her of her 'protective armour'. Up to now, she had been able to rely on this to 'survive' just such situations. By mentioning this, she evoked a feeling of guilt in me of having deprived her of what she needed for survival without providing a substitute.

Now everything threatened to collapse for Mrs. E. The iron slogan *You can, you should, you must!* seemed no longer effective. She was filled with a longing to die and overwhelmed by destructive impulses, feeling a strong desire 'to destroy everything' and to harm herself. When I linked this to our sessions and made the connection with her mother's greedy, envious image, she experienced this as a devastating accusation and at the same time as confirmation of her worst fear, that is she *was exactly like* her mother. But when she missed sessions (for which she always gave me advance notice), and in view of her destructiveness, I felt similarly helpless and powerless, as presumably she must have done (albeit to a much more severe degree) during her childhood.

In a dream she was standing in front of her former school in which a fire had broken out. The fire brigade had come too late and looked at the immense devastation. Her classmates' charred bodies sat on the chairs and she wished that she could have burnt and died with them.

In view of this burning destruction, I felt impotent, as if I had 'arrived too late', like the fire brigade, and maybe was even responsible for the devastating fire, which had erupted in her.

Only now did it become clear to me to what extent her own destructive powers were bound up in her pathological organisation and I began to doubt whether the treatment could extinguish the fire it had ignited. This danger was real but nevertheless I thought that the desperate situation in which we found ourselves had probably been unavoidable if anything was to change at all.

Mrs. E. seemed to sense that I had a rest of confidence left over. She asked me what made me hang on to the treatment so tenaciously. At the same time, she expressed her dependency on the sessions as never before. On one occasion, she expressed this dependency on me with the image of a 'puppet on a string'. On another, she said that there was 'no way back now' and she hoped that *I knew what I was doing*. I felt the responsibility she handed to me, but was full of doubt and did not know myself how things would turn out.

A phase of coexistence

A new situation developed from these difficulties in the subsequent months. Mrs. E. returned to work, but could not function as 'perfectly' and impersonally as before. She began to develop a trusting relationship with one of her managers and an older female colleague. For the first time, she allowed herself to take small meals during working hours, discarding her previous rule to not eat for at least 17 hours during the day. In the analysis, too, she seemed to be able to take up more of my interpretations rather than just experiencing them as criticisms or 'orders'.

This somewhat freer handling of her life was reflected in therapy, where she arrived a few minutes early or was dressed in casual clothes for her session (whereas she used to be dressed in work clothes, which she referred to as her 'uniform'). While waiting, she could allow herself to lean against the back of the chair. She could begin the session by simply saying that she had enjoyed something, or was sad or did not know where to start. She seemed less preoccupied with what I expected of her and I, too, felt more at ease to share my thoughts with her.

Despite all the difficulties in the marriage, she had decided to stay with her husband. She encouraged him to seek therapy and during this they got closer to each other. For some time, they had taken in two kittens and shared the responsibility for these two 'cat children'.

Despite all this, the 'men in the tower' remained as punitive background figures. They warned her 'not to go too far', reminding her of 'her duties', but accepted her analysis in order to 'make her a better person'. Conversely, she no longer had the feeling that I insisted on a complete renunciation of these contacts or else I would no longer be available to her.

Thus, a peculiar sort of compromise had developed in which parts of her pathological organisation continued to exist while being able to make use of the analysis in her life. This coexistence allowed her to enjoy small liberties such as inviting a girlfriend, going out with her husband or trying new cooking recipes, all of which made her feel a hitherto unknown joy of life for brief moments. Until then, the only justification for her existence had been to 'survive in order to function for others'.

These small liberties were 'good' and 'real', showing the limited but real changes she had been able to make with the help of her analysis.

This was a challenge to the splits between 'good' and 'real', 'bad' and 'unreal'. She realised that there were experiences which had good *and* bad aspects and were nevertheless 'real'. In this way, she was able to take more responsibility for the good as well as the bad inside her, instead of declaring it unreal, or turning it into devastating self-accusations or else act out in the form of self-harm. The patient had the impression that she was changing and that this process was irreversible. But these changes were still unstable, and in view of the freedom they afforded her, obviously very limited.

Further changes

Nevertheless, I had the impression that Mrs. E. could make better use of her analysis. She developed a palpable dependency on the sessions accompanied by a sense of gratitude, no longer solely based on submission. But she remained anxious and fearful that something 'might happen', and that everything she had worked for would be lost, for instance by me leaving or something happening to me. On one occasion, she believed that my facial expression was sad when I greeted her and she raised this directly with me. On another occasion, she saw my bunch of keys in a different place than usual and became anxious that I was going to leave after the session and not return... Eventually, she voiced her anxiety and alarm regarding a long break (of three weeks) and gratefully accepted my suggestion to contact a colleague of mine during this period.

All these experiences gave an indication of the important and real experience that her therapy had become for Mrs. E. Her internal voices no longer denounced therapy as 'luxury' to which she was not actually entitled and the daydreams of the cruelties in the 'tower' faded into the background. Instead, dreams emerged depicting particular events of her childhood, which overwhelmed her with intense emotions. She spoke of these dreams as 'memories in feelings', which brought to my mind that Melanie Klein had used the very term when she wrote about 'memories in feelings' (Klein 1957, p. 180).

Her life history no longer seemed an unreal film to Mrs. E. Numerous details emerged, accompanied by great sorrow and anxiety as well as murderous hatred. Only now, so it seemed, was it possible to 'remember with emotion and meaning' (see O'Shaughnessy 1999) and the picture of her mother was no longer entirely deleted. She appeared in her thoughts as the 'chaos monster', or as the 'evil queen' or else as the limitlessly humiliating, self-destructive woman, whom she could no longer help.

She remembered that she had once deliberately tried to get her feet, caught in the spokes of the wheel while sitting on the bike behind her mother, in an attempt to kill her. I learned from Mrs. E. that her father had also had relationships with other women and that these violent and promiscuous affairs of both parents were conducted in plain view of the children. The events in 'the tower' could now be understood as part of a cruel primal scene in which she was not just the victim of perverse men, but the excluded third party, who, while 'knowing everything', was powerless to intervene.

These brief vignettes give an idea of the direction in which Mrs. E.'s internal world developed as the cruelty of her super-ego gradually decreased. Nevertheless, I shared her concern that all might be lost and she could sink back into chaos as being justified and real.

Conclusion

To conclude, I would like to summarise my impressions of the first three years of Mrs. E.'s analysis as follows. On the basis of a catastrophic life history, the patient had developed a complex defensive organisation in which her persecutors had become her 'best friends'. They would offer support and security if she was prepared to relinquish her own life and submit to their torment.

The price to pay was high, but as long as she submitted to the demands of the organisation she was protected from persecution and abandonment. At the same time, she could accommodate her own anxiety of destructiveness and unbearable feelings of guilt in this pathological structure, which fostered an addiction-like dependency on idealised destructive objects. Meltzer (1968) and Rosenfeld (1971) spoke about the complex functions of intrapsychic 'mafia organisations', which seems an apt description of Mrs. E.'s 'men in the tower'.

The problem was that these experiences had been so *real* in her life. For many years, she had been abused by a severely disturbed mother who had handed her over to paedophile men. The survival strategies she had developed in those circumstances, such as not to feel, not to think and most of all to subjugate herself to anything demanded of her (reminiscent of the accounts of victims of torture, see Amati, 1987), had become indispensable elements of her defensive organisation (see Bohleber 2000; Brown 2005; 2006).

With this internal attitude, she entered analysis experiencing my interpretations as criticisms and 'orders'. Mrs. E.'s initial aim was to submit to my demands and to become the way I wanted her to be, in order 'to survive and function', as she put it. In this way, she erected a new 'tower' within the analysis. I had difficulties in assuming the role of such a cruel super-ego feeling encaged in her 'tower' and confronted by my own potential cruelty. But as long as I was only 'good', the analysis remained an unreal experience in a desolate and ruined world.

In the subsequent treatment period, a conflict of loyalty between the analysis and the 'men in the tower' emerged. They seemed to fight each other and to battle for domination. This process evoked rescue fantasies in me. At other times, I felt I was the person outside the tower, who knew and had to witness everything, but was not allowed to intervene. Her 'friends', who were always at her disposal, seemed to be superior to me and more than once I felt powerless and helpless. During this phase of treatment, Mrs. E. experienced an agonising inner conflict.

In this context, internal and external changes induced a transient breakdown of her defensive organisation. Her iron discipline, her 'protective armour' as she referred to it, ceased to function. The 'men in the tower' were no longer available to her. In this phase, she felt beleaguered by chaos and confusion, akin to the 'chaos monster', which terrorised her from within. She experienced a strong desire to destroy, and feared 'going mad'. At the same time, she felt desperately dependent on the analysis. In this state of paranoid-schizoid disintegration, everything seemed to perish and Mrs. E. said to me 'I hope you know what you are doing!'.

Finally, I described a fourth phase in which the remains of her pathological organisation were newly assembled.

In her paper 'A clinical study of a defensive organisation', Edna O'Shaughnessy (1981) has described a similar development. In her case, a highly organised defensive organisation broke down only partially after a period of anxiety and confusion and continued to coexist alongside a split-off part of the patient's personality which had developed a deeper contact with his own feelings and external reality. After this re-assembly, the organisation no longer exerted such an addictive pull over the needy parts of his self. Instead, it served as a transient refuge at times of distress. According to O'Shaughnessy, the persistence of such splits is a typical part of the treatment process.

In Mrs. E.'s case, the result was a sort of 'coexistence' between the modified organisation and her analysis. The organisation allowed her to make use of it in order to become a 'better person', on the understanding that the analysis would not enforce too radical a change in her. One could describe this as the politics of appeasement. It had the effect that small liberties were possible, allowing for 'real' and 'good' experiences, thus gradually undermining the *pathological split between reality and morality*.

The progress made possible by this allowed psychic development. The archaic super-ego, represented by the 'men in the tower', seemed to be replaced, step by little step, by a less pathological structure which permitted *reality orientation*. Melanie Klein has described this process in detail (Klein 1958), as illustrated in the previous chapter. Even if there is an evolution in the super-ego structure, which facilitates a transition from persecution and revenge to genuine reparation, she nevertheless assumes that parts of the primitive super-ego coexist side by side with healthier parts of the personality and that the archaic 'terrifying figures' in the 'deep unconscious' (p. 241), such as Mrs. E.'s 'chaos monster', persist lifelong relatively unchanged.

I would like to add to Klein's thoughts that it is possibly not only for the archaic 'bad figures' but also for the elementary 'good objects' to reside in the deep unconscious. Mrs. E. seemed to have some such capacity to access and make use of the few good experiences that were available to her. Her sincerity and trust, which she brought to our enterprise, impressed and touched me from the very beginning. Even though there were not many good experiences in her life history, she seemed to have been able to retain a capacity for gratitude which helped her (and me, too) to sustain difficult periods in the analysis.

This touches on the question of the relationship of gratitude and reparation, which I will take up in Chapter 7, and on the role of processes of inner integration and reparation in the working through of traumatic experiences. According to Klein, the gradual consolidation of good internal objects contributes to a capacity to deal with the dangers emerging from the deep layers of the unconscious, without causing widespread disintegration, even when the 'terrifying objects' re-emerge at times of extreme 'internal or external pressure' (Klein 1958, p. 243).

What form can reparation take when a child has been exposed to such devastating experiences as Mrs. E.? What is the significance of the recovery of parts of the self, which were lost through excessive projective identification and which role does the struggling with feelings of mourning and guilt play? These questions will be explored in the following chapter in the context of Mrs. E.'s further analysis.

Chapter 5

Trauma, reparation and the limits of reparation

After three years of analysis, Mrs. E. had reached a state of relative stability, which was based on a coexistence of her defence organisation and her newly gained freedoms. This allowed her more flexibility in her relationships with other people as well as towards her own feelings. But although her range was greater, it was still limited. It was based on a decreasing cruelty of her super-ego, represented by the 'men in the tower', which made her feel less persecuted. But as long as she found herself in this kind of in-between position, no real reparation was possible and it was unclear whether this was a permanent state or a vantage point for further development.

The question as to how processes of reparation emerge in severely traumatised patients, and where their limits are, is not an easy one to answer. For such a process to take place, the individual is confronted once again with her or his damaged inner world, which is sometimes devastated and dominated by feelings of loneliness, emptiness and despair. If it is possible to traverse these bleak areas of the human mind, painful feelings of mourning and depressive guilt emerge. This is because in phantasy the individual always feels responsible for the damaged state of his or her internal objects, regardless of whether they have been introjected as cruel and bad figures, of whether they have been damaged by the hatred directed against the good object or because of a combination of different factors.

In any case, to enable movements towards a better integration, projections have to be withdrawn and split-off parts of the self and the object have to be brought together. Only then is it possible for processes of reparation to be activated. Occasionally, this process gets stuck somewhere along the way. This is the case particularly when feelings of guilt have assumed a concrete and overwhelming quality, so that they cannot be worked through, but are turned towards the self in the form of self-accusations and self-harm. In this way, the movement that began as an effort at reparation is turned backward by the grinding gear of the repetition compulsion. Some patients thus remain caught in self-hatred and persecutory guilt. The borderline between good and bad appears blurred, leading to disorientation (Money-Kyrle 1968), confusional states (Rosenfeld 1950) and agora-claustrophobic anxieties (Meltzer 1966; 1992; Rey 1979). Sometimes, the patient attempts to free himself from this situation by discharging unbearable feelings or seeking refuge in abnormal, arbitrary processes of splitting, in an attempt to get rid of the confusion and to bring order to the chaos (Rosenfeld 1964a, p. 218; 1964b; 1965; 1978). The splitting between reality and morality is an example of this.

In such circumstances, reparation seems difficult. Where is reparation going to lead, if the good is just an illusion; if the damage done to the patient in their early life is so 'real' that it can hardly be distinguished from their internal phantasy objects? Many of these patients are entangled in identifications with perverse, traumatising figures. Frequently, these objects are idealised in order to escape from primitive persecutory anxiety and fears of fragmentation. In these cases, pathological organisations are brought into play, which form a 'second skin' (see Bick 1968; 1986; Brown 2005, p. 400) by offering security at the cost of change and psychic development (Steiner 1993).

This is the kind of organisation Mrs. E. developed, where in her imagination she either withdrew into a dark dungeon in which she was imprisoned, or she was cruelly tormented by the 'men in the tower'. In the first two years of her treatment, it had become clear that these internal figures were based on a re-working of the violent, traumatising experiences of her childhood. The persecutors of her childhood and adolescence had later been transformed into her 'best friends'. However, as protectors, they demanded the high price of unconditional subjugation to their principles and thus controlled her life. In this way, they obstructed the working through of mourning and guilt.

This raises the question as to what extent reparation is possible in severely traumatised patients. Can we talk about 'reparation' in someone who has been exposed to such devastating experiences in their childhood? How can we interpret cruelty without re-traumatising the patient and making them feel their most appalling experiences were their fault? Is there a way to understand guilt without re-projecting it into the patient, distorting their past and playing into the hands of their inner self-accusations? And finally: to whom or what should we make amends? To the past or to the present? To internal or external objects? Or to one's own self?

All of these questions have been raised recurrently in the history of psychoanalysis, as mentioned in the introduction. But alongside the theoretical aspects detailed there, there are a number of practical questions we need to think about when it comes to dealing with this dilemma *clinically.*

Should we simply acknowledge what has happened to the patient and confirm their point of view without interpreting the unfolding of the inner scenario and its re-enactment in the transference? Or would we, in this way, only further reinforce the split between good and bad, internal and external, past and present?

But if pathological splitting and the repetition compulsion can only be overcome by reparative attempts, *what form can 'reparation' take in severely traumatised patients?*

In his late work, Herbert Rosenfeld (1987) pointed out the central role of the analyst's counter-transference. It forms the eye of the needle through which the difficult emotional experiences of the patient have to pass to enable a true processing and understanding. If the analyst does not take notice of his own emerging feelings and regards them as a necessary part of an internal process, 'patients like this are unable, when they are alone, to experience anxiety and guilt in a way that enables them to work through this problem' (Rosenfeld 1987, pp. 252–253).

If the analyst lacks awareness of his counter-transference, he is likely to shove his feelings back into the patient (see Chapter 3). Without acknowledging this, interpretations can be used as a defence against the unbearable in the patient (see Brenman Pick 1985; Segal 1997a). In this way, the analyst becomes enmeshed in constellations, in which he either takes on the role of one of the patient's internal figures or becomes identified with a part of the patient's self. To a certain degree, such re-enactments are unavoidable and can even be the pre-condition to gain access to the patient's internal world (see Grinberg 1962; 1968; Joseph 1971; 1985; Sandler 1976; Jacobs 1986; 1993; Feldman 1997; Steiner 2006b). However, when they get lastingly established, they easily lead to impasses, obstructing further development. Rosenfeld (1987) regards the persistence of splitting, which impedes the onset of processes of reparation as an example of this.

Rosenfeld comments: 'It is only when the good and bad feelings are able to come closer together, through a lessening of splitting, that depression, and with this normal thinking and reparative impulses and function, can develop.' (Rosenfeld 1987, p. 251). In his view, good and bad feelings can only come together if this process is mirrored in the experience of the analyst and linked together in the analyst. The presence of the analyst is thus of immediate importance in overcoming splitting:

> It is essential for the patient, therefore, to have the help in the analyst's presence. The anxieties which the patient expresses have

at first to be brought together in the *analyst's mind*, and he has to experience for himself what it feels like to be anxious, concerned, and depressed. It is also essential for the analyst to recognize the importance of first making the effort himself to bear the patient's anxieties and to remain in contact with both his thinking and his feeling. Only then can he gradually start to replay the problem back to the patient in a way the patient can understand and use.

(Rosenfeld 1987, p. 253)

Initial situation

The processes of splitting were only partially overcome in Mrs. E., although she no longer split between 'good' and 'real'. But different perceptions of the same reality persisted side by side, mirroring either the attitude of her pathological organisation or of a part of herself which had developed with the help of her analysis. But it was this seemingly unambiguous coexistence which blocked further integration.

As long as this coexistence continued and the contradiction was suppressed, there was relative stability in the status quo. At the very moment, however, when she was no longer able to maintain these alternative attitudes and experienced their inner contradictions, feeling the clash of her different constructions of reality, she got into desperate states of hopelessness. She was then caught in a cycle of melancholia, loneliness and guilt, with no idea of how to find a way to get out of this dilemma. For as long as her internal world was dominated by vengeful, damaged objects, no further development could take place.

The 'Joan Rivière dilemma'

This kind of hopelessness with no way out was described by Joan Rivière (1936) in detail in her paper on the negative therapeutic reaction. She conceptualised this state as an underlying internal situation *in which the individual can neither repair nor escape their damaged internal objects.* The patient fears that everything they love is dead and destroyed within them:

> (…) all goodness is dispersed, lost, in fragments, wasted and scattered to the winds; nothing is left within but utter desolation. Love brings sorrow, and sorrow brings guilt; the intolerable tension mounts, there is no escape, one is utterly alone, there is no one to share or help.
>
> (Rivière 1936, p. 313)

In such moments, feelings of guilt can become so overwhelming that patients lose confidence in their own capacity for 're-creation and reparation' (ibid., p. 149). At the same time, they fear that every failure and every collapse will bring them closer to the threshold of madness, so that 'inner reality might become real through the analysis' (ibid., p. 148). This is why the treatment is feared, but at the same desperately needed.

I would like to call this internal situation the 'Joan Rivière dilemma'. In Mrs. E.'s case, this meant that her getting into hopeless and seemingly inescapable states was because of the progress she had made in her analysis.

She believed, for instance, that she would never be able to overcome the murderous hatred of her mother. At the same time, she feared that the analysis would confirm her unconscious conviction that she *was exactly like her mother*, one reason why she never wanted children of her own. Furthermore, she was convinced that the abuse of her childhood could never be repaired, which, of course, is true in the sense that it could not be *magically undone*. But it was these beliefs which impeded a healthier integration of her self.

In this way, she was identified with a depressive, guilty mother, as expressed in the image of the dark dungeon. In order to escape from this dungeon, she had to take refuge high up *in the tower* with the sadistic men, where she was exposed to endless punishment, because for a long time, the only possibility to gain access to anything good had been the belief that she had to take on the cruelty of others in order to be 'cleansed'.

As long as this split was operating, it was difficult to make movements towards reparation. Nevertheless, Mrs. E. had made significant progress after three years of analysis. Her 'protective armour', as she called it, her military discipline, her control and readiness to submit, all of this had broken down and made her more vulnerable towards feelings of confusion, sadness and helplessness.

After the marital crisis mentioned earlier, she and her husband got closer to each other again and decided to stay together. They adopted two kittens, which they regarded as their children. This experience challenged her identification with a depressive, guilty mother and led her, without being aware of it, closer to *an appraisal of good and bad* in herself as well as in others. I will go on to show that this motion contained a certain form of reparation towards her own self as well as towards her image of a murderous, guilty mother.

Further developments

This motion occurred at a time when we had applied for an extension of the financing of her analysis by her health insurance. As opposed to a previous occasion some 18 months ago when we were confronted with the same question, we could discuss the issue this time without her being *convinced* that by raising the theme I was trying to get rid of her. She asked me openly whether I was prepared to go on with her, and when I confirmed, she decided to continue without hesitation. She seemed grateful for my willingness to continue with our work and was even prepared to pay for one of the three weekly sessions in order to extend the duration of her treatment.

This straightforward decision was followed by a familiar retreat into self-accusations and bodily complaints. She said she felt worse, as if something had collapsed inside her, and added:

> I can't do it (…), I have already lived too long (…). There is something in me which is part of me and not part of me, which thinks that I only have a right to live if I feel bad.

I tried to link this with her decision to continue with her analysis and her self-accusation that she was a 'bad person' who did not deserve that, touching on her anxiety that everything could easily be lost. To which she replied, 'Ending makes everything seem unreal. If a friend goes away, I believe that I have never meant anything to him'.

I suggested that she was asking herself whether the continuation of her analysis had any personal meaning for me and she replied 'It's your profession. One shouldn't attach oneself too much to a firefighter or to a policeman whose job it is to help in a professional way'.

In this way, she reminded me of my professional duties and rejected my assumption that she wished for personal attention. After a short pause, however, she added that she feared to 'infect' me with her madness and to lose me like her husband and her kittens.

Following this session, she continued attending, but did not go to work and expected me to get annoyed and reproach her for her withdrawal. This, too, was an interaction we were familiar with from previous occasions. Finally, she did go back to the office and, rather unusually for Mrs. E., a conflict developed between her and her older female colleague in whom she trusted and to whom she had confided parts of her traumatic childhood history. This colleague had a daughter around her age and seemed to represent a rather benign maternal figure, together with the head of her department who figured as a benign and protective father.

Material from a session

She began the following session with the remark that she was consumed with anger about her older colleague. They had talked about some male colleagues who regularly came over to submit forms for signature to get paid by the company. The older colleague had remarked 'I know they prefer to talk to you.' That had made her angry, because, she thought, the colleague implied she entertained a special relationship with them and would even talk to them about her behind her back. To that, she had curtly stated 'You know I would never stab you in the back.' But the colleague had perceived the sharp undertone in her voice and said 'We should talk about this again on Wednesday.' Mrs. E. was sure that her colleague was going to discuss this incident with her husband on her return home. He was generally helpful, she said, and added 'he will not fuel the fight but take a neutral, understanding position.'

This open expression of anger in Mrs. E. seemed quite unusual to me. It seemed to be related to the allegation the colleague had made implying that she had a special relationship to the men in the department, which took place behind the colleague's back. But she also had an idea how the conflict could be resolved.

I therefore suggested, 'Your colleague is taking her anger home to her husband and you are discussing it with me here. Perhaps you hope I won't fuel this dispute either', and then I added she might also fear that I, like her colleague, have thoughts about her relationships with the men in her department behind her back.

She then referred to previous remarks I had made, which actually did sound as if I held the same opinion as her colleague, that she was trying to attract the male employees' attention. This led on to the issue of jealousy, particularly the idea that her colleague might be jealous of her for having such a good relationship with the male employees. She responded that she had not even allowed herself to have that thought. I supposed what seemed so unthinkable to her might be the thought of a mother-prostitute nourishing herself by exciting the attraction of the men around her.

To this she responded in a very straightforward way:

> Yes, this is absolutely true. But I am not getting too close to them. It's not true that I entice them. Some of them are friendly and I talk a bit with them, but never about any personal issues because work is not the place to do this.

I said perhaps she was describing her difficulties with me here in the consulting room, especially if a more personal relationship developed and she wouldn't just see me as a firefighter or a policeman. Trusting someone, like her colleague or me, would make her feel very vulnerable and would be terrible if not requited.

Discussion

I suppose with my comment regarding her difficulties in trusting people, that there could be a mother who would not stab her in the back and a father who would not stir up arguments, I took on a calming attitude, which did not immediately address the anxiety provoking vision of her relationship with the men in her department and the reaction of her colleague. However, when I put my assumption to her that she feared that I, too, might have thoughts behind her back about her relationships with her male colleagues, a disturbing version of the oedipal situation was addressed where she was identified with a mother-prostitute and I with the male colleagues in her department with the 'older, female colleague' standing for the excluded child of the primal scene.

This version was brought home to her with my interpretation that she was possibly disturbed by being identified with the image of a mother as prostitute, who is nourished by the excited attention of the men. She had to dispel this suspicion by emphasising that it was not true that she wanted to seduce anyone.

This made me feel that I had gone too far, as if I were 'infected' by her disquiet. So I left it at that, continuing in the role of fireman, policeman, professional father in order to calm her disturbing thoughts. But then it became difficult to 'talk about things and sort things out' as her colleague had said. Thus we were left in a position where crime, 'infection' and guilt were not easily to be addressed and worked through, maybe because the 'contact barrier' between us had become too permeable in this moment (Teising 2015, p. 106).

Nevertheless, something had come to life in this session and a degree of reparation could take place. Mrs. E. was angry with her colleague and presumable with me because of my remark. She was indignant about the suspicion in the room that she had entertained special relationships with the men in her department. Nonetheless, she responded to my interpretation that she feared to be identified with her mother as a prostitute and let me know that something could quickly became 'infectious' as soon as a personal relationship developed. And last, but not least, she had talked about human emotions, such as affection, disappointment, jealousy and anger. But this atmosphere changed when she came to her next session.

Material from the next session

On entering the consulting room, I instantly noticed a change in Mrs. E.'s mood. She was dressed entirely in black and with her long, blond, cascading hair she floated towards the couch. After lying down a long, soft silence spread. After a while she said, as if talking to herself, in a quiet voice, it would be better to stay silent today. And after another silence she added 'Today is a day where I do everything wrong!' She let me know that she would prefer to stay silent rather than talk.

I responded that as long as she remained silent, she could do nothing wrong. Maybe if she spoke with me everything might just get worse.

She responded saying that she had had the feeling at work today *to be different from all other people*, adding:

> I am not allowed to make mistakes like others. A mistake by me would be unforgivable. This is one of the days when I feel I have no right to be in this world. I have to start all over again and again, I am not allowed to make mistakes.

While she spoke, my mind went to the odd way in which she had come into the session with these floating steps. I said she saw herself full of badness and mistakes. The only creatures who were absolutely 'pure' and flawless were angels. Maybe behind the conviction that she was bad, she had the idea that in order to do no wrong she had to be like an angel, which indeed would make her 'different from all other people'.

She said that she had been unable to talk to her colleague after yesterday's argument. She was sure that the colleague thought badly of her now. But she could not afford any more mistakes. She added that she was convinced that her colleague had spoken about her to others and had let them know that she could not be trusted.

I commented that she seemed to think the very thing about her colleague that she accused her to think of her, namely to talk about her behind her back, a comment that shocked her at first.

After a short pause she replied 'In a way that's right. But when you say that I see myself as the morally superior person… it's different for me, I have no right to be here if I do not fulfil the expectation of others.'

I asked her what she made of my comment that a part of her which was not allowed to make mistakes felt morally superior. To this she responded 'It's as if you had said that I should stop feeling so special, arrogant and superior'.

I put it to her that she had evidently heard my comment as a moral criticism. Her feeling of being 'different from other people', not being allowed to make mistakes, to be silent rather than speak had evoked the image of an angel in me, full of anxiety of 'falling' and thus becoming the bad person who drew the attention of her male colleagues onto herself and talking behind her female colleague's back.

There followed a somewhat long silence in which I began to feel that *I had done something wrong* by insisting on my observation. The mood was tense and I feared that I would lose contact with her.

I therefore decided to take a step towards her by saying that the atmosphere of today's session was quite different to the preceding one. Then, she had talked in a lively way about human conflicts dealing with jealousy, deceit, trust and anger. At the beginning of this last session, she had been disgruntled, but had had hope of clarification, as her colleague would talk to her husband and she would talk to me. But this seems to have changed. Now, there was a tense silence with everyone being anxious not to make a mistake.

There was another silence of nearly ten minutes.

Eventually she replied in a slightly livelier voice:

> When I was silent, I thought my head was empty, filled with cotton wool. Then I remembered a situation at work today. Three of us were to have a meeting with the male colleagues of the other department. My two female colleagues talked about various things they wanted to raise. Then one of the male colleagues asked me what I wanted to address and I said 'nothing'. He was surprised as I usually have a lot to talk about.

A short silence followed.

Then, I said that at the beginning of the session she had said that she had 'nothing to talk about', did not wish to be in contact with me for fear of making a mistake or that anything she said was going to be used against her. She felt confirmed in that when I talked about the image of the angel, which she heard as a kind of mockery or moral criticism on my part.

She replied 'On such days I don't know who I am. I have no history, no memory of my self and no feeling for myself'.

I replied 'Quite different to the last session'.

To which she said 'But today everything is erased. I don't see myself as an angel. What I have in mind is the image of a charred body. A black lump of coal with a few sparks still smouldering.'

I remarked 'The opposite of an angel – dead, burnt, abused, rather like hell than heaven'.

She quickly added 'Invulnerable!', and I said that she had to become this unreal, faultless person to not crash down into hell.

In a much clearer voice, she now added that she had always believed that she came from hell, and that she had no right to be here among people, as she only brought harm.

I was surprised and asked her where this conviction came from.

She said she could put an exact date to this. It was when she was admitted to hospital, aged 11, close to starvation. There, she was seen by a psychologist who did not say anything to her and when she asked her mother afterwards, she explained 'He said you have a *black soul*'. From this moment onwards, she had known that she came from hell.

This was the end of the session, which she left in a significantly changed mood compared with the beginning of the session.

Discussion

One striking feature of this session was the change of atmosphere compared to the previous session. It seemed as if Mrs. E. had left the human world of conflict to enter a moral universe where she seemed difficult to reach and every contact implied the danger of moral fault.

She had had 'nothing to say' at the staff meeting with her male colleagues just as she had stayed silent with me. Contact was dangerous, because 'mistakes' could not be forgiven and perhaps I had made such a mistake when I had spoken about the imagery of the 'angel' which had occurred to me as she entered the session. She seemed to experience this as a moral accusation telling her she should finally stop feeling so 'special', 'arrogant' and 'superior'. This, in turn, made me feel that I had gone too far and the subsequent silence gave us a glimpse of what it meant to feel entrapped in a world filled with accusation, failure and guilt beyond repair. In this state of mind, the world is divided into black and white, unreality predominates and reparation seems well-nigh impossible because of the splitting.

How had this dramatic change in the mood of these two sessions come about? It seemed to me as if an envious figure had entered the scene, suggesting to my patient that she was not allowed to live in a human world of conflict. An overwhelming concreteness had taken hold of her, perhaps partly as a consequence of my speaking about her fear of being identified with a mother-whore. She might have experienced this *not as an interpretation, but rather as a factual statement.*[1] Similarly, my mentioning the imagery of the 'angel' might have reactivated some early reminiscences of her childhood abuse. This left her forced to choose between 'good' and 'bad', which was being equated with the idea of having to live either in 'heaven' or in 'hell'.

As long as she remained silent, she could freeze her human feelings. But it was exactly this frozen world of morality which made movements towards reparation so very difficult. Nevertheless, after a long silence which at first seemed 'empty', the patient was able to let me know about her problem of getting in contact with me during this session. By bringing in the picture of the charred coal still smouldering, she helped us to imagine the picture of hell as the place where she believed to have come from.

This brought some sparks of life into the session and allowed us to address more realistically the difficulties in our relationship. When she was admitted to hospital near starvation at the age of 11, the psychologist's silence was translated to her as having a 'black soul'/coming from hell. I thought by mentioning this memory, she let me know that she took in my interpretations in a very *concrete way* at times, hearing them as judgements rather than as attempts to understand her internal world which was so concretely present for her. By giving me this hint, some hope re-emerged that the deadly silence of the beginning of the session could be overcome at some point.

The subsequent sessions

This spark of life was, however, short lived and in the next session Mrs. E. let me know that the link between her mother speaking of her 'black soul' and her own conviction to be 'dark, buried and coming from hell' had made her feel even more despairing. She said she had been thinking about suicide or cutting herself and also of asking me for the possibility of an extra session. Bringing the two sides in her together, her wish for life and her longing for death had been almost unbearable.

I replied that she had heard my interpretation, like the silence of the psychologist, as confirming rather than relieving her guilt and therefore had returned to her addictive suffering and self-punishment. As I said this, I felt my frustration and anger about her rejection of my work.

This anger got worse when she complained again about her older colleague in the subsequent session. Because of a cold, she had not been at work on Monday, but had phoned in to ask her colleague not to create disorder by 'leaving loose leaves' on the desk. The colleague had reacted angrily and simply stated that she hoped she would not continue to be absent so often and that she sometimes found it difficult to work with her in the same room. Mrs. E. was shocked by this reaction. Had she not told her colleague about her disastrous history? But the argument between them escalated and the colleague even said, 'Even if fate burdens you with bad experiences, one day you have to stop the suffering'. She even added, 'I think you would be healthier and not fall ill so often, if you could finally forgive your mother!'

That really annoyed her and she thought, 'That's how easy it is... But I *cannot* forgive my mother, I hate her... If forgiving means, it's all right, it doesn't matter... But it *did* matter to me and it still matters to me'.

Hearing about these arguments, I could sympathise with her colleagues' anger. I was impressed by the unconscious significance of her statement that for as long as she could not make reparations, she had to suffer. At the same time, I thought that my patient was right in saying 'I cannot forgive my mother, I hate her.'

So it was difficult for me not to take sides. I felt the dilemma between empathy and anger, between compassion and reproach and tried to remain balanced by interpreting that her hatred was not only directed against her mother but also against herself when she felt simultaneously guilty and identified with her.

At the same time, I doubted whether this intellectual and somewhat helpless interpretation could actually reach her, and therefore I added that with her hatred and suffering she was also attacking the goodness inside herself. Maybe she could not forgive her mother, but it might be possible to acknowledge that her mother must have been very ill.

After this intervention, I felt uneasy about my attempt to limit her self-hatred and to find a realistic and acceptable form of forgiveness for her. When she left the room, she cried and also my anger had now turned into sadness and dismay. I informed her that the insurance had approved the prolongation of her treatment. But I also had doubts whether our work made any sense and whether her internal world was damaged beyond repair.

The following session

She came to the next session full of terror and despair. She burst into tears and asked me whether she could sit today, something that had not happened before. In a broken voice, she said 'Something terrible has happened!' One of their two cats had fallen off the balcony and had died shortly after. She sighed and was hardly able to let me know that she felt terribly guilty because she had let the cat wait for too long on the balcony. Suddenly, a bird had landed on the banister and the cat had jumped up onto it. When her husband hastily opened the balcony door at that moment, the cat startled and fell off the third floor. She hurried downstairs and found her cat with twisted limbs on the floor. She died on the way to the vet.

While Mrs. E. talked in a faltering voice, her narration was disrupted by animal like screams and she sobbed several times 'I have lost my daughter, oh, my poor little girl!'

Seeing her in her despair was moving but difficult to bear. Appalled by the sudden loss and overwhelmed with sadness and guilt, she repeated that she could not lie down on the couch today, just as she had been unable to sleep the night before, because her body felt 'twisted' when she lay down. She looked at me with tears in her eyes and said she feared to overburden her husband with her wailing.

At this moment, she appeared to me very little. Her sadness and helplessness spread inside me. I thought, perhaps, she needed someone like her husband to take in her sadness. At the same time, I thought that it would make little sense to console her or to appease her feelings of guilt. Therefore, I just tried to describe that she seemed to come to this session like a 'kitten-daughter' hoping there would be some space for her sadness, that she could 'sit' and I would not let her fall, like the kitten from the banister of her balcony. I added that her screams sounded like coming from a cat and that her body felt 'twisted' like the body of her kitten when she had found her dying on the ground.

It seemed difficult to address her feelings of guilt, but the element that made them almost unbearable was that they were connected with loving feelings towards her kitten-daughter. I tried to address this and kept in mind that at this moment *she was identified with a guilty rather than with a murderous mother*. But in this session, I felt I could only just acknowledge how sad and desperate she actually was. Nevertheless, she seemed a bit calmer when she left the room and expressed some relief that she could return for her following session the next day.

Additional thoughts and further developments

It is difficult to evaluate what Mrs. E. evoked in me when she came to the session in such a desperate state. She could not 'rescue' her kitten-daughter just as I was unable to 'rescue' her. I felt sad and helpless, but not desperate. In this moment, Mrs. E. seemed to be simultaneously identified with a guilty mother and a lost child. Her cat-like screams and her repeatedly saying 'Oh, my little girl' expressed this vividly, and the overall mood was obviously different from the withdrawal and cold hatred of the previous sessions. This change brought her to the limits of what she was able to bear and perhaps also me to the limits of what I was able to take in and to contain. This seemed to be reflected in her fear she could 'overburden' her husband with her moaning and my struggling against an internal impulse to console her and to absolve her from feelings of guilt.

But it was exactly the acceptance of guilt which would enable further development. During the first weeks, this seemed almost impossible since the session after the death of her kitten was one of the last before the Christmas break. She felt reminded of scenes of her childhood and expressed her belief that all would come right if only her kitten would come back, crawl between her and her husband and sleep at her feet when she lay in bed. In great detail, she told me stories from the life of her kitten as if intense remembering would allow, at least for brief moments, to make her alive again. But she also knew that the loss could not be reversed and she refused her husband's proposal to adopt another kitten before Christmas. She had never been as sad as this before in her life.

After the Christmas break, she fell ill and did not return to her sessions for several weeks. Time and again she phoned to apologise and to let me know that she was 'still ill'. When she returned, she appeared weary and withdrawn. It took me some time to realise that during the break she had experienced my absence as if I had let her fall.

When I addressed this, she slowly emerged from her withdrawal. She told me that she had locked herself up at times for fear of being pursued. Then, her sadness had returned. She could not prevent herself from weeping in the office and her colleague tried to help her to deal with her sadness and feelings of guilt. After three months, she and her husband decided to adopt a new kitten. But the new kitten was different and could not replace what she had lost. Once again, she felt sad and guilty, but at the same time some appetite for life emerged. For the first time since her wedding, she spent a brief holiday with her husband and this encouraged her to develop a sense of appreciation and protest. In the sessions, she would now sometimes disagree with me and in doing so she realised that something must have changed.

These changes, however, were brittle and fragile and if something went wrong, she easily fell back into resignation and self-doubt. Nevertheless, she let me know how much she needed the sessions and thereby expressed a simple, but undisguised feeling of gratitude. This implied an acknowledgement on her part that the damages and losses in her life could not be undone, as well as an acknowledgement on my part that the effects of the analysis would always remain limited in comparison with the experiences she had undergone.

Reparation, mourning and guilt

Reflecting on this development, I thought Mrs. E. was now able to conceive of a feeling of guilt that was not entirely devastating and beyond repair. The relationship she introduced to the session was no longer the relationship between a *murderous mother* and a *dead child*, but rather between a *guilty mother* and a *lost child* – perhaps in search of a husband/father who could take on the horror of her loss. This enabled her to mourn and to struggle with her feelings of guilt that were no longer experienced as so persecutory and unbearable. Clearly, this meant a movement towards the depressive position, i.e. a step out of her 'dungeon' to face the reality of mourning and loss.

As she continued to insist on hating her mother, her reparation was not primarily directed towards the hated object, but towards that part of herself, which was unconsciously identified with a figure devoid of any human feeling of forgiveness and guilt. Therefore, I think that reparation in severely traumatised patients remains *always incomplete* and relates primarily to parts of the patient's self.

Mrs. E. expressed this clearly in her complaint 'I have lost my daughter, oh, my poor little girl!' At the same time, she addressed her sudden mourning at a third object, her husband, me or a father-figure who could perhaps take it in and by doing so prevent her from an excessive identification with a persecutory maternal object. It was predominantly Segal (1991; 1997b; 1999) who pointed out the function of the father as someone setting boundaries. This has the effect that a state of *separateness* is introduced in which depressive feelings can be lived through and do not have to be defended against in a paranoid way. In this way, Mrs. E. had moved away, at least temporarily, from the desperate situation described by Joan Rivière, where no hope of reparation exists and thus the only remaining alternative is 'death or madness' (Rivière 1936, p. 314). To put it in terms of her psychic retreat (Steiner 1993), she had left her 'tower' of cruelty to move into the 'dungeon' of her depression and departing from there regained a capacity to deal with the reality of mourning and loss.

One could speculate as to what it is that is actually damaged by the traumatic experience. Maybe the damage is not just to the developing psychic structure, but to the integrity of exactly those processes of reparation, which *under normal circumstances enable reparation* in the individual. As with modern oncology, the focus would then not be on the direct structural damage, but instead on the damage to the repair mechanisms and processes (such as apoptosis, for instance) which prevent the unhindered proliferation of destructive forces. Analytically, this would mean *to acknowledge* the damage done to the patient in the past, and predominantly help him/her to regain a *capacity for reparation* in the present.

Looking at it in this way, *overcoming the 'repetition compulsion'* (Freud 1914g; 1920g) means *the reinstatement of reparative processes* as they appear step by step in the transference and unfold gradually in the analytic relationship. Roger Money-Kyrle (1956) addressed this when he wrote that the patient's damaged internal objects are being taken in by the analyst and transformed in his/her counter-transference. He talked about *a slow-motion process*, which is subject to being easily disturbed and happens in countless little steps. In as much as the experience of *being understood* precedes the possibility of active understanding, the likelihood of reparation is linked to the analyst's capacity for reparation of their own damaged internal objects and to *forgive* the patient, who comes to represent these objects (see Weiss 2003; 2012b).

Only then can the analyst feel empathy, 'acknowledge the countertransference and reflect it in the service of the patient and thus in the process of reparation' (Özbek 2015). As discussed in previous chapters, the emergence of a benign super-ego is a pre-condition for such a development to come about.

Mr. D. (Chapter 3) could not overcome his grievance as long as he projected his failure into others and acted like a merciless, angry superego. Mrs. E., however, blamed herself for everything and tended to punish herself. For as long as she was caught up in her frozen, moralistic world of ruthlessness and self-accusations she could not make reparations. This universe was characterised by a *static balance* in which she and her internal objects could only be in 'heaven or hell'. In 'heaven', unreality predominated and the slightest mistake would lead to a fall from it. In 'hell', she could neither make reparations nor escape her damaged internal objects. In my view, this dilemma corresponds to the desolate situation, that Joan Rivière (1936) has described so vividly in her paper on the negative therapeutic reaction. As long as she remained there, she was addicted to suffering and experienced my interpretations as incessant moral criticism. In this agonising place, she felt secure in as much as she knew about her 'badness', but was cut off from reality and any kind of psychic development.

During the course of her analysis, Mrs. E. gained a growing capacity to leave her psychic retreat. In such moments, she felt sadness and guilt, but also appeared to be more lively and able to face ordinary human conflict. This became evident in her arguments with her colleague, in the way she experienced the loss of her cat and finally by no longer agreeing with everything I said. In this way, her gratitude became more real (see O'Shaughnessy 2008) and reparation was no longer equated with submission, which had, up to then, been her only possibility to survive in a cruel world. Despite all difficult circumstances, she could imagine for the first time becoming pregnant and in one such moment had the thought that to bring a child into this world would be a 'reparation' in relation to her life.

In the beginning of Mrs. E.'s analysis, such moments were limited and could easily switch back into the familiar state of 'omniscient despair' (Britton 1998). Evidently this had happened during the

Christmas break after the death of her kitten. But in the following phase of analysis, she recovered and regained a capacity for reparation. The adoption of the new cat was not just a substitute for what she had lost. It created a space for mourning and new life and at the same time a new capacity for remembering emerged.

Final remarks on remembering and forgetting

This form of remembering was different from the traumatic flashbacks of her childhood at the beginning of her analysis. It is interesting to ask the question how the capacity to repair is linked to a developing capacity to remember and forget.

In his late work on remembering, forgetting and forgiving, the French philosopher Paul Ricoeur (2004) described a form of 'retaining' or 'containing forgetting', which is different from the traumatic recurrence of the past as well as from the 'destructive forgetting', which erases the imprints of the past. The latter 'effaces' the imprints of the memory itself, obliterating everything as expressed by the old metaphor of imprinting on a wax seal, described by Plato and Aristotle (Ricoeur 2004 p. 13).

This form of *obliterating forgetting* is different from the forgetting that even in its repressed form retains the imprints of the past and can therefore be returned to. Looking at it in this way, it might be said that traumatic experiences have the effect of *switching off the containing forgetting* by creating a kind of hollowness or vacuum in the human soul.

This vacuum is then filled with '*traumatic remembering*' as I would like to call it, a kind of memory, which is not genuine remembrance, but more of an *overwhelming of the present by the past*; a state in which we remain trapped in endless repetition without being able to forget. It is because the 'containing forgetting' is no longer possible that the individual is caught in the ban of an eternal present, in which the experience of time dissolves.

In his reflections on '*containing forgetting*', Ricoeur (1998) converges with the philosophy of Martin Heidegger, who in his work *Being and Time* (1927) described *Gewesenheit* (*the past that has passed*) as a state of current absence and thus a pre-condition for remembering and memory.[2] One has to be able to forget in order to remember, and where one cannot forget, one cannot remember, but lives in the ban of eternal presence, which never passes. In this way, so Ricoeur, 'there also exists a reserve of forgetting, which can be a resource for memory and for history' (Ricoeur 2004, p. 284)[3], a reserve which may have to be reconstructed in severely traumatised patients such as Mrs. E.[4]

Ricoeur (2004, p. 457) links this process with what he refers to as *difficult* or *'heavy forgiving'*, where 'mourning can be compared to the work of remembering' (ibid. p. 72), not a complacent forgiving, nor a benevolent or lenient forgiving, as these would all be within the logic of retribution, but what is needed instead is a new working relationship towards *guilt and loss.* As he puts it, 'The work of mourning is the cost of the work of remembering, but the work of remembering is the benefit of the work of mourning' (ibid. p. 72).

Ricoeur finds an allusion of such a process in Hegel's concept of 'reconciliation' as 'mutual acknowledgement' (Hegel 1807), which always has to open up a position for a third party or an 'Other'. It is only this third perspective which allows for a gradual overcoming of the circularity of the friend/enemy thinking, the world of dead ends, where there are only perpetrators and victims. It is in this sense that Schöpf (2005, p. 165) speaks of the 'relationship opening significance of a third perspective'.

Perhaps this relative heaviness and slowness of the processes of reparation is the reason why analysis takes time. But it is not time alone that enables reparation and a *remembering with emotion and meaning*, to achieve this, the dimension of subjective time has to be regained. This is a central theme in the literary work of Jenny Erpenbeck's novel *The End of Days* (Erpenbeck 2014), which will be examined in the next chapter.

Notes

1 I am grateful to Franco De Masi (Milano) for this idea.
2 'Just as expecting is possible only on the basis of awaiting, *remembering* is possible only on that of forgetting, and *not vice versa*; for in the mode of having-forgotten, one's having been "discloses" primarily the horizon into which a Dasein lost in "superficiality" of its object of concern, can bring itself by remembering' (Heidegger, 1927, p. 389).
3 Bion is said to have remarked that for every memory there must be something forgettable (personal communication, David Taylor, London).
4 Aleida Assman refers to the interwoven relationship between remembering and forgetting in her book 'Forms of forgetting'. She distinguishes between an 'automatic' and a 'containing forgetting' as well as 'selective', 'punishing', 'defensive', 'constructive' and 'therapeutic' forgetting (Assmann 2016).

Chapter 6

Traumatic remembering and ecliptic forgetting

On the riddle of time in Jenny Erpenbeck's *The End of Days*

Throughout her work, Jenny Erpenbeck grapples with the riddle of time, not unlike W. G. Sebald, who in his essays describes a clotting, obliterated time in which the history of the individual gets caught, as if in a labyrinth – an experience in which time is transformed into space and thereby becomes haunting (Sebald 1997, 1999, 2001). Not least because of his writing style (Fuchs & Long 2007), Sebald takes a melancholic view of history in its pervasive belief in progress[1] (Barzilai 2007), whereas Jenny Erpenbeck describes the *sensual composition* of time, the viscosity of its passing, the uncanny repetitions, the gentle unreality that goes hand in hand with the standing still of time and the panic and dismay in the face of its transience.

In this way, she lets the reader take part in an experience in which we as clinicians are frequently placed when listening to traumatised patients. The 'numbing feeling of reality' (Bion 1961, p. 149, see Steiner 2011b) arising in the listener corresponds to an inability in the patient to dream when they are asleep, and to be awake without being haunted by nightmares (see Brown 2005). Instead of dreams, concrete pictures arise in which perceptions, memory fragments and ideas are linked together in such a way as to pull us in as if under a spell, and to paralyse our capacity for thinking. The analyst then experiences a feeling of 'immediate reality'. While the patients describe their experiences, he gets sucked into their reality and eventually becomes 'unable to remain open to perceive the underlying unconscious communications' (Steiner 2011b, p. 78). Without noticing, the analyst begins to perceive, feel and react as if he had become part of the patient's internal world, and it takes a while to emerge gradually out of this experience and to notice how caught up and ensnared they are. It is only when the analyst re-awakens from his counter-transference feelings, that an observing stance can be recaptured and a return to symbolic thinking can take place. Jenny Erpenbeck's novels expose the reader to some extent to such an experience.

In her debut novel *The Old Child* (Erpenbeck 2006), she describes a girl who has fallen out of time. One day, she is found in the street, empty bucket in hand, without a history, identity or memory. She is taken to a Home, where she lets herself be dealt with passively, without any internal participation, with 'flawless inward submission'. The Home functions like a shell, an external wrap into which the girl slips for want of an internal space. As long as the girl practices 'the art of forgetting', sinking into passivity and timelessness, she is protected from anxiety, pain and envy, but most of all from getting older. Everything is static, everything is virtual, nothing has meaning. Time stands still. It is only when she wakes from a dreamless sleep in which 'childhood was a thing bobbing upon a vast ocean of time' (ibid., p. 74) that the first fragments of memory emerge. In this moment, an unappeasable sadness sets in, in which the girl, by now already a grown woman, regains her identity and history: 'She was bumped up against time like a blind person, at this she has to weep. And the hand she always used to blow her nose with is as heavy as lead, she cannot lift it' (ibid., p. 100). In the clinic to which she is admitted 'it is reported how often the patient is now seen to weep, she weeps even when her eyes are closed, in sleep, her prank has flopped, her attempt to stop time in its tracks has failed' (ibid., p. 107).

Visitation (Erpenbeck 2011), which was originally published nine years after *The Old Child*, deals with the fates of people across generations and times who are connected with each other by a house, a garden and a lake. In this novel, she considers the concurrence of things which always remain the same as they are, and of experiences which never recur as they are past.

In her novel *The End of Days*, Jenny Erpenbeck (2015) returns to these themes in a renewed form linking them with each other in a complex way. Her narrative can be read in different ways. One can understand it as a retracing of the great tragedies of the 20th century from the perspective of different people over several generations, which introduces us to the family history of the writer Hedda Zinner, well-known in the GDR and the grandmother of the author. However, Jenny Erpenbeck's novel is much more than this.

To start with, it is the history of a life which has hardly begun, ending in a sudden infant death and re-starting four more times; a life which begins at the onset of the 20th century in the small town of Brody in Galicia and ends in Berlin in a re-united Germany; this life, four times disrupted and four times re-started, as if each beginning were destined to end in a renewed tragic and mostly violent death. If the parents had known that the sudden death of a child could be chased away with a handful of snow, the family would not have broken apart and the daughter would have moved to Vienna with her parents at the end of the First World War. Had she not crossed a frozen puddle in the wrong direction in that wretchedness, she would not have met that unhappy lover who ended their lives in a joint suicide. Instead, she would have joined revolutionary circles, emigrated to the Soviet Union where she would have died of hunger and cold in a Stalinist labour camp. If her file had not landed on the wrong pile with the secret police, she would have returned to Germany after the war and become a celebrated author of the proletarian revolution. And finally, if she had not been killed in the 1950s by falling down the stairs, she would have experienced the German reunification, only to die two days after her 90th birthday in an old people's home in Berlin from dementia.

All of this could have happened – or not. If coincidence had moved fate in only a slightly different direction, everything could have been different... The linguistic form of irrealis ('what would have happened if...') serves the author as a literary device to develop a story in which the beginning comes back to the end and the end comes back to the beginning. In this way, the reader is presented artfully with the interplay of cultural and contemporary history, of familial and personal enmeshment. However, I still think that Jenny Erpenbeck's novel exposes us above all to a disturbing experience, even more so than her earlier works *The Old Child* or *Visitation*.

The more the reader gets involved in the story, gets roped in so to speak, the more they lose track of where they are. Maybe Jenny Erpenbeck's novel cannot be read without being touched and confused in this curious way.

It is at this point that the reading becomes interesting for the psychoanalyst. It is as if the differences between before and after, between inside and outside, between fiction and reality and between the self and the other are constantly shifting. Then, there are these constant repetitions. Lives ending in sudden infant death, in a joint suicide, in falling down the stairs, in being beaten to death or in being hastily buried in a labour camp, as if the experience of change dissolved in time, as if that *which would be memory in different circumstances* is all of a sudden *concrete experience*. An experience which comes from the future into the present breaks into it without any chance of escape, as if there were neither mourning nor forgetting, as if the inner space in which experiences can be ordered in time were missing. The repetitive theme is that of recurrence and impending catastrophe – a catastrophe which actually has already happened and therefore cannot be escaped.

If we compare time, according to a familiar metaphor, with a flowing river, then the reader of this novel, just as the main characters, will be swept along by the current. There are moments when the stream of the narrative is quietly running along, only to form currents and eddies that pull one in and then one drowns and re-surfaces and finally ends up in those areas of stagnant time, which W. G. Sebald (2001) described as 'lagoons of forgetting'. It is this remorselessness and relentlessness of time, its harshness and also its softness, akin to water, which is the central theme of Jenny Erpenbeck's book. This great novel about the riddle of time is also about the *regaining of memory*. Memory which cannot be thought of for a long time because it is circling in repetitions, has gone astray and gone the wrong way, because, as she writes 'time is like a briar that has gotten caught in wool' (Erpenbeck 2015, p. 228).

It is exactly because time gets entangled with the external events time and again that it cannot turn into the continuity of a story. For this reason, the baby who dies at the beginning of the book is not really dead. As sudden and unexpected as this hardly begun life ended, it recurs in the different destinies the author goes on to describe. One could read these destinies as a concatenation of dreams or as one long dream. But this possibility of seeing the events as if from outside is blocked for the reader for a long time. The experiences Jenny Erpenbeck unlocks by means of her language are too concrete so that the reader cannot escape. 'Words themselves were reality' and 'was it the case that reality itself consisted of words now?' (ibid., pp. 144, 145). In this way too, her novel brings to mind Sebald's tales *The Emigrants* (1997) or *Austerlitz* (2001). It is no coincidence, just as the supposed coincidences in her story confirm fate, that the author prefaces her book with a quotation from Sebald's *Austerlitz*, 'We left here for Marienbad only last summer. And now – where will we be going now?'.

What was before and what is later, where is the 'here' and where is the 'there' – all this seems to dissolve just like the identity of the people who are drifting in the current of events. It is this *dissolving of time*, the *suspension of boundaries* which has the effect that a person can always slip into another. As the author puts it in the second part of her book:

> Why was it not possible for her to love her friend and also her friend's beloved; what exactly was being forbidden her, and by whom? Why was she not permitted to plunge into love as into a river, and why, if she was forbidden to swim in these waters, was there no one else swimming there?
>
> (Erpenbeck 2015, p. 101)

And when this young medical student in the third semester whom she hardly knows, shoots himself together with her, the novel continues with:

A dead woman has infinite relatives; she is now infinitely loved and can love anyone she likes, all the while dissolving entirely, with her dead thoughts, in all the others. Did anyone ever see such soft lips on a man before? She now floats upon these lips utterly interspersed with the one she loves, drifting far away, the two of them are the water and also the dark blue sky above it, and all who were trapped behind the two endless rows of windows have now flung them open and are breathing deeply in and out.

(ibid., p. 102)

Here, the experience of death does not mean the limit of life or the sadness about an irreversible loss. On the contrary, it becomes the 'beginning of immortality', a threshold to a world without limits and without endings. Slipping into another space, another body blurring into one.

In psychoanalysis, we call this experience by the somewhat cumbersome name 'projective identification' (see Frank & Weiss 2007). This refers to processes whereby parts of ourselves slip into the other unnoticed, insert themselves there, invade another person's mind to control them from inside just as we, in turn, are overwhelmed by and caught up with them. These experiences often reside beyond words or more precisely, before, next to and under words, like a melody surrounding us without us ever being able to get away from it.

I think that Jenny Erpenbeck's language gets close to these original emotional experiences, experiences the child has long before it is capable to use language in a symbolic way. Donald Meltzer (1983) has called this level of early exchanges between mother and child 'vocalisation' as it pre-dates the 'verbalisation', the speaking in words. It is the larva stage of unconscious phantasy, in which *meaning* is directly contained in *sensory impressions* (Isaacs 1948; Weiss 2014a), in experiences of words, sound and gesture, which hold an overwhelming concreteness. 'Words were something you could touch', as she writes (Erpenbeck 2015, p. 131). Words which are:

> ... just as real as a bag of flour, a pair of shoes or a crowd being stirred to revolt... Van Gogh had cut off his ear, why shouldn't it hurt just as much when a figure in a play cut off someone else in the middle of a speech?

(Erpenbeck 2015, p. 131)

The author conveys these experiences through the precision of her language as well as through the slowness of her prose, the interrupted sentences, the inserted dialogues and the many repetitions in her text.

Freud (1920g, p. 41) referred to this as the 'vacillating rhythm' ('Zauderrhytmus') of life, which he closely associated with the 'fate and repetition compulsion'.

The repetition leads to an *agglutination of the past with the present and we can neither forget nor remember*, because the possibility of remembering is tied to the experience of sadness and loss. When this path to sadness and mourning is blocked, the past hangs about the present, like a fog that clouds reality.

It is striking that Jenny Erpenbeck's characters remain nameless for a long time and do not dream until almost the end. One could therefore try to read the whole novel as a dream of terrible experiences of loss, which cannot be mourned, of memories which remain frozen for a long time and only break out towards the end of the novel, like 'a curtain suddenly ripping in two' (Erpenbeck 2015, p. 195).

As long as this curtain blocks the view of reality, 'time is a porridge made of time, it's rubbery, refuses to pass, has to be killed, spent, served, and still keeps dragging on. (…) Then the iron reserves make their appearance (…) The iron reserves, fear' (ibid., p. 219).

Towards the end of the first part of the book, which is in five parts, Jenny Erpenbeck recounts how in the face of such catastrophic experiences of loss – the tearing apart of a family – everything that could have been pain, sadness or guilt in other circumstances, suddenly dissolves into concrete bodily experiences.

> One hand pulls a sheet taught, another wipes crumbs from the table, a third flips a light switch. One pair of eyes sees dust motes rising in a beam of light, another peers into men's wide-open mouths (…). Ears hear a door being slammed, sirens, someone coughing; feet slide into silk stockings, elbows are massaged, toenails are cut, filed and polished (…), grey, black, brown hair; rings under eyes; calluses; two weary breasts; almost a proper bald spot; toothache; tongue; a voice like silk. *What under other circumstances might have been or become a family has now been torn so far asunder that being drawn and quartered by horses would be nothing in comparison.*
>
> (Erpenbeck 2015, pp. 53, 54; italics mine)

From clinical experience, we are familiar with such states of splitting and internal fragmentation. Their effect is that they dissolve not just the feeling for the self, but the relationships with our internal figures into a concrete, part-object experience, resulting in persecutory, confusional states accompanied by diffuse anxiety or agonising depressive feelings.

These states are evocatively described in *The End of Days*. The running out of breath, the freezing, falling down the stairs, falling out of the world, falling out of time and finally the image of a sphere 'with perfectly smooth, black walls, and you keep running and running and there isn't even a shabby little door to let you out' (ibid., p. 96).

One cannot imagine a more evocative description of a depressive experience. As indeed there is no getting out of the dark prison of timelessness for as long as one carries stories inside oneself, which neither let one go nor can be told.[2] This is because, as the author explains, 'when he slipped out of his mother's womb, he was already filled with interior spaces that did not belong to him, and he can't just look inside to inspect his own interior' (ibid., p. 224).

Sigmund Freud (1916–17g) expressed this in the poetic metaphor of 'the shadow of the lost object' that falls on the ego. Today, with Jenny Erpenbeck, we would more likely say that the ego is ensnared with an internal object (Meltzer 1992), which it can neither leave nor mourn (Steiner 2014).

Instead of experiences in time, there is a frantic wandering in a labyrinthine space, in which, as in the 'black sphere', one returns time and again to the starting point without noticing. From our experience with borderline patients, we are familiar with feelings of being enclosed in these states of mind (Weiss 2009). As long as one wanders about in this labyrinth, one can indeed not 'see' one's internal space. One lives in a psychic retreat (Steiner 1993), in which every new experience ends in a return of the same.

To get out of this state, one has to relinquish the *concrete possession of the object*, letting it go to be able to mourn, as is described in the last chapters of *The End of Days*. All of a sudden, the son begins to dream, recognises his father again and is gripped by a fierce sadness. 'I dreamed that I was dreaming. And suddenly it was no longer a dream' (Erpenbeck 2015, p. 236). In this moment in which the curtain of forgetting is torn, he is immersed in the experience of time. As this happens, the recognition of his father and the sadness about the death of his mother seem like an awakening after a long dream. Because only at the point of space and time where we can remember do the experiences of the past become real, and only then the present regains its life with all the losses, which cannot be reversed and have to be mourned. For is it not the truth that what has happened can only have happened if we are able to think it (see Weiss 2005)?

Jenny Erpenbeck claims that she has never concerned herself with psychoanalytic theory in any detail.[3] Nevertheless, she seems to have intuitive access to the questions which concern us in the context of time.

Therefore, I would finally like to direct my attention to the description of remembering, forgetting and forgiving in *The End of Days*.

Erpenbeck speaks of a *loneliness*, which evokes a particular form of forgetting, namely when we are *too close* to what we might remember, so that it ends up in a 'blind spot'. It is the darkness of the internal space, which produces this form of forgetting, which is fundamentally different from that which we commonly call repression.

I would like to call this form of forgetting *ecliptic forgetting*, because, as in an astronomical eclipse, a present object is shifted in front of another, which is therefore no less present, but invisible. Unlike Freud's 'repression', 'that ingenious form of retaining forgetting' (Lang 1978, p. 125), and also different from the state of unconscious remembering, of which Hegel (1830) says in his *Encyclopaedia* that it is like a 'nightly shaft in which a world of infinite pictures and ideas are stored without being conscious of them' (§ 452 Z), ecliptic forgetting corresponds more to an *empty space*, which is filled with the presence of the virtual real. This *traumatic remembering* is different from the 'return of the repressed' because as yet it has no space in which it could be thought of. Is it a memory which is hallucinated, or a hallucination which masquerades itself as memory?

In an imaginative synthesis, Leonard Weiss (2016) has retraced the connection between Freud's theory of remembering and forgetting and what Hegel called 'the night of consciousness'. In both, so he concludes, it is the reference to language which brings back the unconsciously remembered to the reality of interpersonal communication (ibid., pp. 236–238).

In contrast, what I call *ecliptic forgetting* is rather far removed from the symbolic world. It *dwells* in the body (like Mrs. E.'s serpent) or in the concrete perceptions of the external world. It is less of an archaeological site rather than a vacuum in the human soul or, to speak with Jenny Erpenbeck, a stillness, which is filled with concrete impressions:

> … that mutely lay or flowed within the earth: the springs, the roots, and the dead; the cry of the cuckoo off to one side would be just as real as the stones crunching beneath the sole of his shoe, as the coolness of evening and the light falling through the leaves to the ground before him, as his hand that he is using to stroke his mother's back, feeling her bones beneath her thin, old skin, bones that will soon be laid bare – briefly, sharply clearly, he knows for one instant what it would feel like if the audible and the inaudible, things distant and near, the inner and outer, the dead and the living were simultaneously there, nothing would be above anything

else, and this moment when everything was simultaneously there would last forever.

(Erpenbeck 2015, p. 236)

Precisely to escape from this *eternal contemporaneousness*, 'to see this other world with the eyes of his mother', he has to get away from her: 'I dreamed that I was dreaming. And suddenly it was no longer a dream' (ibid., p. 236).

We would say that every one of us needs to make this effort of leaving and letting go in order to find our place in the world, that we cannot bypass sadness, transience and loss when we cross the threshold of time-lessness and expose ourselves to the roughness of reality, because only then can the lost external object continue to live within us as a memory. For as long as we avoid this pain, our remembering will be mere *traumatic remembering*, a falling out of time and our forgetting will be mere *ecliptic forgetting*.

Ecliptic forgetting is not 'retaining/containing forgetting' as Paul Ricoeur (see Chapter 5) has called it. It is rather 'destructive forget-ting', which erases the traces. Traumatic remembering is *not a realisa-tion*, which brings us closer to the 'forgotten past' (Freud 1914g, p. 150). It is the sheer present, which intrudes raw and unsymbolised into the individual's experience. At the same time, hyper-real and unreal, gentle, confusing or threatening.

Of such a permanent present it already says in Augustine (Book XI, XIV.14), 'this would no longer be time, but eternity'. In order to immerse ourselves in time, time has to sink into the past, has to leave the 'black sphere', to find back to its origin. 'I dreamed that I was dreaming. And suddenly it was no longer a dream'.

How does it come, asks Lawrence Brown (2005, p. 417), that a *flash-back* turns back into a *screen memory* (Freud 1899a) and thus effectively becomes a first step towards the construction of history? In Jenny Erpen-beck, this process begins with the regained capacity for *dreaming*. In *The Old Child*, as well as in *The End of Days*, it is the dream which tears the veil of timelessness and opens up that painful and now irreversible process of mourning and re-appropriation, the sinking into time, which Ricoeur refers to as 'difficult/heavy forgiving' – a forgiving which unavoidably puts us in touch with sadness and guilt, because they form the pre-condition for reparation and genuine remembering.

'I don't know, his mother says, what it can mean that we are so sad' writes Jenny Erpenbeck at the end of her book. In the moment when the telephone rings at six o'clock, the son knows that his mother has left him forever. In conclusion, I end by quoting the last lines of the book:

For one week more he will awaken every morning at precisely 4.17am, every morning precisely at the moment of the greatest silence, just before the birds begin to sing. For the first time in his life, *he will have dreams during these nights that he still remembers when he wakes up.*

His mother is lying just barely underground, her head is still sticking out: Are you the one who was with me in Ufa, she asks. Yes, he answers and lifts up the ten centimetres of earth like a blanket to place a photograph of his two children upon her breast. And then he wakes up, it's perfectly quiet, and then all at once the birds begin to sing, it is 4.17am. Many mornings he will get up at this early hour that belongs only to him and go into the kitchen, and there he will weep bitterly as he has never wept before, and still, as his nose runs and he swallows his own tears, he will ask himself whether these strange sounds and spasms are really all that humankind has been given to mourn with.

(Erpenbeck 2015, p. 238)

Notes

1 In *The Rings of Saturn* Sebald (1999, p. 24) writes 'For the history of every individual, of every social order, indeed of the whole world, does not describe an ever-widening, more and more wonderful arc, but rather follows a course which, once the meridian is reached, leads without fail into the dark'.

2 The one hope the main character in Jenny Erpenbeck's novel has of leaving the darkness of forgetting is writing, because 'there's nothing left for her to hope for now than to succeed in using her writing to write her way back to life' (Erpenbeck 2015, p. 119).

3 Personal communication, 10 March 2014.

Chapter 7

Reparation and gratitude

In his reflections on 'difficult/heavy forgiveness', Ricoeur links forgiveness with the concept of *giving*. In his view, there exists an asymmetric relationship in the exchange between giving and *forgiving* because of the *surplus of the gift* (Ricoeur 2004, p. 148). Giving always remains asymmetrical because it escapes the logic of economic calculation. In this way, it establishes a relationship between the giver and the recipient, which, although reciprocal, is unequal. According to Ricoeur, this asymmetric relationship is at the origin of gratitude. It imparts *generosity* to the giver and leaves the recipient their *dignity*. This forms the foundation of the relationship between giving and forgiving.

In the history of psychoanalysis, gratitude is a concept which appeared relatively late. Melanie Klein introduced it in her paper 'Envy and gratitude' (1957), in which she described envy as a feeling which undermines 'feelings of love and gratitude at their root' (p. 176).

In her paper, Klein describes the different forms of envy, its disguises and concealments as well as its transformations, which may appear as greed, grievance or resentment, as fake modesty or as a constant state of dissatisfaction. She shows how envy may be projected into others, so that it is they who appear to be envious of us. But there is less mention of gratitude, *why* this experience is often so difficult to express and, also, whether there are pathological forms alongside the genuine versions of gratitude.

If we look for that, we can orient ourselves on Klein's concept of 'reparation', developed particularly in 'Love, guilt and reparation' (Klein 1937), 'A contribution to the theory of anxiety and guilt' (Klein 1948) and 'On the development of mental functioning' (Klein 1958). Following her reflections in these papers, gratitude is closely linked to the onset of processes of reparation, by which envy, jealousy and resentment can be overcome when feelings of guilt emanating from the primitive super-ego are no longer unbearable (see Brenman 2006).

Those brief instants when Mr. D. (Chapter 3) was able to leave his desolate island to communicate his neediness and gratitude were examples of such movements. In those moments, he seemed more open, but also more vulnerable.

Instead of paranoid fears and fantasies of retaliation, the need to absorb good experiences emerges, which in turn become the basis for gratitude and generosity. On the other hand, the capacity for gratitude is in turn a pre-condition for reparation and the ability to internalise good experiences (Klein 1957, p. 301). Eric Brenman (2006, p. 149) described this conflict as a power struggle between the primitive super-ego and the possibility of finding access to good experiences. If the latter is not completely blocked, a benevolent cycle of gratitude and reparation can develop and limit the destructive cycle of envy and persecutory guilt.

In this context, the analyst's counter-transference is of supreme importance in containing the angry super-ego that is set on revenge, to understand its importance in the maintenance of a pathological balance and not to take revenge, but modify the pathological structure in small steps (see Chapter 3). This point of view was already put forward by Seneca in his first treatise 'On Anger', where he emphasises that it would be 'a hateful mode of cure to owe one's health to disease' ('On Anger', I, 12). In the third book, he adds that what it is about is that we are content in ourselves and with ourselves.[1] Seneca lists a number of 'wholesome instructions for healing' including deferment in time, renunciation of revenge as well as bearing 'in mind that we are mortal' (III, 42,5).

Primary gratitude

In an observation on the origins of gratitude, Edna O'Shaughnessy pointed out that movements leading to the regaining of good experiences are sometimes evident even very early in treatment, although they can be temporarily obscured later on by negative therapeutic reactions (O'Shaughnessy 2008, p. 80).

A disturbed eleven-year-old boy was sent for psychoanalytic treatment by his parents, who were very concerned about his school performance. O'Shaughnessy noticed that no one seemed to have noticed the young boy's depressed mood. He seemed to have habituated to finding everything 'normal' and she suspected that he tried to avert his anxieties in this way. When she put this supposition to him, he agreed and began to cry. She then spoke to him about his inner sadness and asked him whether the origin of this was unknown to him or whether he knew where it came from. He replied 'The former' and seemed even sadder. In response, O'Shaughnessy said that he wished that his sadness were seen as well as her empathy and the empathy of his parents, but maybe not necessarily a 'psychoanalysis'. Now, he began to look anxiously and curiously around the consulting room and she said that he did not know yet whether he wanted to leave or stay. He nodded in agreement. His anxiety and internal agitation were now clearly palpable and she added that although he was a big boy, he sometimes felt like a small child and he was afraid of her as he did not know what to expect. He nodded vigorously. After saying good-bye, he returned once more crying out 'Thank you. Thank you so much'.

O'Shaughnessy (ibid.) suspects that sometimes gratitude may appear *before* envy and express a readiness to receive something good, as in the case of the 11-year-old Leon, who evidently felt understood in his anxieties and sadness, hence his need not to run away, but to express his gratitude.

In a similar way, Mrs. E. (Chapters 4 and 5) seemed to possess a capacity for *primary gratitude* despite the devastating experiences of her childhood and the power that a pathological organisation had gained over wide areas of her life.

In her essay on the occasion of the 50th anniversary of the publication of Klein's paper 'Envy and gratitude', O'Shaughnessy pointed out that following on from Klein, many more papers were written on envy than gratitude (see Roth & Lemma 2008). Maybe this is because gratitude, unlike envy, is a feeling that can evoke vulnerability and embarrassment, as well as sadness and fear of loss: because in the moment in which we are grateful to another, we have to acknowledge *that we are separate from them*, that we do not own them, are dependent on them and therefore what we got from them is *transient*.

Gratitude in the history of philosophy

In the history of philosophy (see Reiner 1972), gratitude appears in the context of 'grace', 'friendliness' and 'reciprocal kindness'. In the Aristotelian tradition (*Rhetorik*, 1385a 17–24), the latter is only awarded the moral value of genuine gratitude if 'it is not linked to an endeavour to get rid of a disagreeable obligation by this effort of compensation, but is based on a freely giving generosity' (Reiner 1972, p. 9), whereby εὐχαριστία means 'gratitude in word and deed' as well as 'a grateful state of mind' and the knowledge to whom and how to show gratitude (*gratiam referre*) and lastly how to accept gratitude (Cicero, Seneca, Pseudo-Andronicus).

In the Christian tradition, as in Thomas of Aquinas, the idea of gratitude as a 'virtue' (*gratitudo*) emerges, in the sense of there being indebtedness for the kindness that was bestowed. This brings the concept closer to 'justice' and 'duty', ideas further developed by Adam Smith (the balancing *re-compensation*; Smith 1759) and Immanuel Kant (gratitude as 'holy duty', Kant 1797; both quoted in Reiner 1972, p. 12). However, from a psychological point of view, this is problematic as it blurs the difference between gratitude as a spontaneous feeling and 'dutiful gratitude' as a super-ego demand.[2]

Nevertheless, it seems significant that the feeling of gratitude is linked with a fundamental experience of indebtedness in the philosophical tradition too. Christoph Demmerling and Hilge Landweer (2007) put it the following way 'One could almost say [gratitude] assumes the mantle of *slight guilt feelings* hand in hand with *impulses of reparation*, as if one had transgressed life itself and therefore has to be grateful for what one is given nonetheless' (p. 107; italics mine). In a similar vein, Otto Friedrich Bollnow describes gratitude as a spontaneous reaction to a 'gift (…) received without deserving it' (Bollnow 1954, p. 169). It implies a reciprocity where 'a service bestowed is not immediately exchanged' (ibid.) but the freedom of the gift is returned in the sense of a 'retaining memory'.

With this, we return to the Aristotelian concept of gratitude as *a response to bestowed benevolence* (Ross 1925, *Aristotle: The Nikomachean Ethics*, 1133a). This reference to bestowed benevolence (*benevolentia*) makes it clear that the experience of gratitude is closely linked to the experience of being loved. In this sense, the Aristotelian sense, it is 'reciprocal benevolence' as opposed retaliatory revenge. We are grateful vis-à-vis a person who loves us and forgives us our hostile feelings.

Insofar, we could say that our capacity for gratitude originates from our identification with an object, which is able to love and to make amends. Maybe this was in Freud's mind when he wrote 'to the ego (…) living means the same as being loved – being loved by the super-ego' (Freud 1923b, p. 57).

But is gratitude always linked to the appreciation of a loving object relationship? Do we always tend to regard gratitude as an expression of the life instincts such as we usually regard envy as a destructive force?

Pathological gratitude

In her essay on gratitude, as mentioned previously, Edna O'Shaughnessy (2008, p. 82 ff.) mentions a form of gratitude, which she names 'pathetic'. The patient she describes had a tendency to assure his analyst that he was grateful for her work, while at the same time not paying his bills and largely ignoring her interpretations, only taking them up 'gratefully' when they essentially reflected insights he had already gained for himself. This form of gratitude makes a mockery of the concept, because there is something patronising and condescending in it – hence Edna O'Shaughnessy's apt description 'pathetic gratitude'.

I suspect that there are further forms of *pathological gratitude* in addition to the patronising, condescending gratitude of the narcissistic patient as described in Edna O'Shaughnessy's paper: for example, *humble gratitude* which is based on adoration, submission and repressed resentment, or *effusive gratitude,* which contains manic elements by ignoring separation and loss, repaying what is received in exaggerated ways. *Placatory gratitude* avoids anger and conflict; *sycophantic, seductive or hypocritical* gratitude which we see as fake gratitude, as nothing is given in return, because the motivation is to scheme and plot. Finally, we know the gratitude which expresses something obsessional, superior or self-effacing, by portraying itself as assurance of friendship, romanticism or false humility, as, for instance in the statement 'My humility is my greatest pride!'

In the clinical setting, these various forms of gratitude cannot be easily distinguished from genuine gratitude. Perhaps it is because of this difficulty that we react with embarrassment at times when we receive a gift from a patient. In giving us a gift, the patient is provoking a response from us to their gratitude, which inevitably means that we have to express our own feelings. I would like to illustrate this with two short clinical vignettes.

Our reaction to being given gifts

Mrs. F., a romantically melancholic patient, was faced with a break of several months in her analytic treatment with me because of changes in my professional life. In the transference, she idealised and admired me and had avoided any kind of expression of disappointment and anger, just as she had done with her husband from whom she was separated. Instead, she had often emphasised her 'gratitude', particularly at moments when feelings of disappointment would have been more appropriate. To me, this 'gratitude' seemed exaggerated as well as submissive. But I had difficulties to interpret this without hurting her. She did not respond to any of my attempts to address this theme, but instead said that she let my words 'melt on her tongue' while she immersed herself in the sound of my voice. This response evoked feelings of anger and guilt in me.

In the last session before the aforementioned break, she came with an ornately wrapped gift, which I was only to unwrap after the session. It turned out to be an elaborately illustrated coffee-table book on the sinking of the *Titanic*, which annoyed as well as concerned me.

It concerned me because she seemed to experience the break as a cruelty, perhaps like a collision with an iceberg, and it made me angry because her despair and rage had been cloaked in this submissive gratitude, which did not allow for a conflict with her internal or external reality, particularly when it involved feelings of disappointment, anger and sadness. At the same time, the image of the *Titanic* evoked a romantic idea of 'sinking', in which she was not separated from me, and space, time and transience had no effect.

I think that this form of 'gratitude' expressed predominantly a phantasy of not being separate. With her gift, she was ostensibly sinking into me like the *Titanic*, which absolved her from having to deal with the reality of separation and loss. In this way, she could maintain control over her object, while not having to face the pain of separation, but also stifling the possibility of her own development. Therefore, Mrs. F.'s gratitude seemed to express a *'possessive gratitude'*, which could neither relinquish nor receive.

Things were different in the case of Mrs. G., a borderline patient in her mid-30s. She had expressed her anxiety and insecurity from the beginning of treatment, when she told me that she found it difficult to lie on the couch in my presence. She asked 'What animal would expose itself to such a danger in nature?' With this, she voiced her paranoid anxieties right away at the beginning of her analysis. At the same time, she warned me not to intrude too far into her internal world by saying that her 'bodyguards would make short shrift' of anyone attempting that.

Nevertheless, she got used to the couch setting in due course and benefited noticeably from treatment. In her spare time, she looked after a smallholding in which she kept chickens and horses. One day, to express her gratitude, she brought me a present. She experienced this as a delicate issue as she was unsure as to how I would react. In this case, the gift was a few eggs from her biological farm. I accepted her gift and added that it might not just be an expression of her gratitude but also a hint that there was something fragile in her internal world, which, like eggshells, could easily break, if not handled with due care. She was touched by this comment, and after briefly crying she added defiantly that she would bring me something again if she felt like it.

As one can see, the presents of Mrs F. and Mrs G. were quite different as was my reaction to receiving them. Mrs G. was quite concerned about giving me a gift as she did not know how I would react. She was actually quite worried that something could go wrong. By contrast, Mrs. F. was not interested in my reaction to her gift. She wanted me to open it after the end of the session when she had left and the meaning of the gift was evidently to concretely incorporate me into an omnipotent phantasy, like that of the sinking *Titanic*. My voice seemed to sound as seductive to her as the music played on the sinking ship.

Both patients had been exposed to repeated cruelty and humiliation during their childhood years, to which they had reacted differently: Mrs. G. with defiant protest and revolt, Mrs. F. with submission, erotisation and idealisation. Accordingly, they developed different defensive organisations in later life which were mirrored in the transference situation.

Mrs. G. had let me know about her paranoid anxieties and her threats right at the start of treatment. She lay down on the couch 'under protest', just as she received my interpretation about the symbolic meaning of her gift 'under protest'. She said she would 'nevertheless' give me a gift if she felt like it. Her dismay and her protest made her gratitude into something real, whereas the sinking of the *Titanic* was synonymous with a phantasy of melting into unity. Although in some way, Mrs. G. had also drawn me into the idealised 'enclave' (O'Shaughnessy 1992) of her eco-friendly smallholding, in which we both cultivated natural products in a careful and protected way, she allowed me to have thoughts about her gift. In the case of Mrs. F., this was a lot more difficult. I had the sense that I was going to either offend her or else confirm her longing. The latter was reinforced by her *separating the sound of my voice from the meaning of my words*, which she could then take in like a longed-for gift.

Gratitude as acknowledgement and receptivity

I imagine that gratitude is bound up with *receptivity* as well as with an *acknowledgement of separateness*. This realisation of being separate from a person who is important in our life goes hand in hand with painful feelings of vulnerability and dependency. Receptivity implies an appreciation of the loved object on whose love we feel a lifelong dependency.

The gradual realisation of this dependency, i.e. the acknowledgement of good attributes in the other on whom we are dependent without being able to control them, helps to develop an increasing appreciation of separation and difference.

Difference can go hand in hand with appreciation and respect. It can lead to new experiences. But equally easily, it can flip into mistrust and envy, particularly if the perception of difference is bound up with feelings of disadvantage, inferiority and shame. In that case, the original need to be loved turns into disappointment, resentment and vengefulness (see Chapter 2) and the initial receptivity is transformed into a power struggle (see Steiner 2014), damaging the good qualities of the object as well as damaging the needy self.

It is this almost unavoidable constellation which generates feelings of guilt, engenders fear of loss and at best becomes the vantage point for efforts of reparation. These aim to avert the loss of the loved object and to re-establish the internal relationship with it. Genuine gratitude can only set in when efforts of reparation are made, reality is acknowledged, the claim of control and possession of the object is relinquished and the good experience is internalised as part of the process of mourning. This implies the recognition of *separateness and connectedness* in equal measure. In this way, reparation can be compared to the restoration of a functioning 'contact barrier' (see Teising 2015).

Accordingly, gratitude originates in the efforts to make reparations and the motive for reparation is guilt.[3] This allows us to restore the internal relationship to our love object, which is now given autonomy and independence. Only then it becomes a figure we are dependent on, in whom we can recognise good as well as disappointing qualities, who loves us but will also continue to disappoint our omnipotent demands.

This becomes particularly evident in child development when the father or a sibling appears and the 'special' relationship with the mother is put into question. In this situation, it will become evident whether or not the internal relationship to her is good enough to weather such disappointments or else the relationship will be spoiled by indignation and jealousy. It is for this reason that gratitude is incompatible with feelings of resentment, envy and contrition as well as excessive shame. It is often those feelings that are in the foreground when attempts at reparation fail (see Chapter 2).

However, gratitude is more than just overcoming resentment, envy and vengefulness. In its essence, it is a *reciprocal relationship* and therefore assumes that something can be given back in return. The need to give back goes beyond the readiness to forgive and to pardon. Gratitude as *requited benevolence* (Aristotle), as opposed to vengeful retaliation, originates in our wish to bestow our appreciation for what we received. This wish is based in our identification with an object that is capable of love and reparation. In this sense, gratitude implies the acknowledgement of difference as well as the readiness to give and receive.

'Enjoyment', says Melanie Klein, 'is always bound up with gratitude; if this gratitude is deeply felt it includes the wish to return goodness received' (Klein 1963, p. 310).

However, what is given and what is received in return is rarely concurrent or equivalent. Here, too, difference plays a role which presumes a capacity to tolerate diversity and to *wait* (defer gratification) and thus limits our wishes to give *everything* and owe *nothing*. The unequal distribution of needs, abilities and possibilities leads to an experience of inequality, which is experienced as painful, particularly at the end of treatment, and may re-activate defence mechanisms thought to have been overcome. Analyst and patient then realise that the separation has a different meaning for either of them. Often it is this difference which gives cause to feelings of mourning.

Mourning is bound up with relinquishing omnipotence and accepting reality. It would probably not be too far off to say that the gods are as incapable of showing gratitude as they are of being able to learn from experience. In the world of human experience, however, it is sometimes difficult to recognise manifestations of gratitude. Genuine gratitude need not be emphasised or affirmed, but is frequently expressed *indirectly* as *psychic development*.

All of this has been illustrated in the above-mentioned philosophical deliberations on the phenomenon of gratitude, but it is clinical experience which amplifies it. Only this can shed light on the underlying conscious and unconscious motives. I would therefore like to go on to illustrate some aspects of the development of gratitude as well as showing the difficulties relating to the expression and recognition of it, using the example of the end phase of a psychoanalytic treatment of a female psychotic patient.

Clinical material from the analysis of a psychotic patient

Mrs. K. was in her mid-50s when she came for treatment, having experienced a psychotic hallucinatory episode followed by a long-lasting depression, which was accompanied by ongoing psychotic symptoms and threatened to permanently undermine her professional performance as a lecturer in a college of higher education (see Weiss 2013). When she was not plagued by her persecutors, she experienced an agonising depression and emptiness, as if she did not know who she was, where she belonged and where she was going. When she began treatment, she said she felt like 'a nutshell drifting aimlessly in a sea of timelessness'. It was this state which left her helplessly confused or else exposed her to dangerous turbulences in which she feared to drown.

In the course of her seven-year psychoanalytic therapy, she managed to gradually overcome her ruptured internal world, which had formed the basis of her psychotic turbulences. For a long period of time, she had wrestled with persecutory and punitive internal figures, which terrorised her from inside and, in the first years of treatment, threatened to regain the upper hand, particularly during treatment breaks. During such periods, she experienced me as an agitating, persecutory or else redeeming figure or she retreated into a time capsule, which she called 'hibernation'. In this state of 'hibernation', she could survive breaks in therapy, to emerge subsequently from her frozen, timeless state to thaw out and bring her confusing feelings and thoughts, which she called 'visions', into our relationship which in the beginning of treatment were hardly distinguishable from hallucinations. Even though she experienced my interpretations as 'pretty crazy' at times and was annoyed by them at other times, she once told me that she had 'the greatest respect' for my continuing endeavour to explore her internal world. She said she was irritated by my interpretations, but added that, somehow, they 'seemed to be helpful' because they reduced her acute persecutory anxiety. In this way, we developed a trusting relationship which in due course allowed us to explore and understand her primitive psychotic anxieties. The patient described her treatment as a 'container' and wondered what others might think about her if they knew about all the 'crazy things' she discussed with me. Professionally, she had re-started her teaching with a lot of personal investment and feeling somewhat burdened by the work, but had nevertheless earned her colleagues' respect and her students' gratitude.

During the treatment, both parents of the patient died – the father at the beginning, when she was still quite psychotic, and in the sixth year of treatment, the mother, whose death made her feel intensely sad. In the beginning, she had experienced her mother as a split figure who pursued her during the day with cold 'doll's eyes' while rocking her into a redeeming sleep at night. As the treatment progressed, her own conflicting feelings regarding her parents came to the fore and she could increasingly experience them as figures separate from her and linked with each other. As her splitting and projection of both love and hate feelings decreased, she could regain lost parts of herself. At the same time, she began to make efforts at reparation, being no longer blocked by paranoid feelings of guilt. Similarly, she experienced me as someone who had helped her find a way out of her madness and was therefore important to her, but at the same time she occasionally felt disappointed by me, which triggered dissatisfaction and anger in her.

For a long time, no further psychotic states had occurred in the transference, while the patient increased her circle of friends and successfully did her teaching job. Nevertheless, she feared that these changes were not sustainable unless her treatment continued *endlessly*. Why should she give up something which had become such an integral part of her life and which gave her a feeling of security?

Nevertheless, a feeling had grown in her that she would have to leave eventually to live her own life. The idea of the inevitability of leaving was linked to her sadness about the death of her mother. She often revisited the places of her childhood, the orchards and fields surrounding the farm where she had grown up, to remember her parents.

In this period, she had brought herself to the decision to end her sessions in the spring following her mother's death. This decision had not been easy at all and she asked whether she could come back if things went awry. The end of treatment coincided with the end of her teaching contract in the following year and she pondered various ideas as to what she might be doing afterwards.

The last treatment sessions

I would like to go on to present material from the last four sessions, in which the patient became painfully aware of the inevitability of the ending and the feelings this evoked in her.

In the *fourth* session before the ending, she said that she was sure that she was going to be sad at the very end of her treatment, but that she was also confident that she would internally retain something.

Then she mentioned that she had to get an MOT for her almost eight-year-old car and maybe she should take it to 'Mister Wash', a car cleaning outfit, so that it would make a better impression during the inspection.

I commented that she might feel uncertain how I would judge her state of mind and her development after almost eight years of analysis. She did not want to leave a bad impression on Mr Wash/ Mr Weiss. Maybe she also had the wish to make my work look good and unsullied by disappointment and doubt. If she got through this inspection, so she hoped, she could internally retain something and be on her way.

She responded by saying that I was very friendly to her, but she wondered whether it was just a relief for me that my work with her would soon be over, like she felt at the end of a strenuous academic year. While her students left a familiar institution heading for a new and uncertain future, she was looking forward to the break and continued just the same the following semester with the next course. She suspected that it was exactly the opposite here.

I commented that it was obviously important for her to find out how I felt at the end of our shared work.

She reacted in a slightly embarrassed way by saying that she sometimes wondered whether the separation meant anything to me, whether I had personal feelings or whether I just continued my work with the next patient on the next course. She was sure she would visit the clinic on occasion to see how things were developing, but such thoughts made her feel sad and evoked embarrassment.

Then, she left a lengthy pause and proceeded to tell me of a 'project' which she and a girl friend had started a few weeks ago. They had rented a garden plot and, together with the gardener who looked after the land, had thought about what to plant: vegetables, berries, fruit to be harvested in the summer. The work was progressing nicely and it reminded her of her childhood and her parents' farm. If they had a good harvest, she might even be able to sell some in the market.

I was touched by this idea of which she had talked about for some time and asked her to tell me more about her plans. At the same time, I felt reluctant to interpret her activities, as if I had the feeling, I was putting her to shame or taking something away from her by doing so.

For the *third* last session on a Monday, I arrived nearly ten minutes late. She was sad and annoyed, reproachfully saying did I have any idea what this meant for her as I only seemed to think of my own work. I felt guilty, but did not want to explain the reason for my late arrival as I thought she was justified to feel annoyed. I added that my lateness seemed to have reinforced her doubts as to whether her leaving affected me in any way. Somewhat defiantly, she then told me about her teaching and that she had had a good weekend. Towards the end of the session she said that she was sad about leaving.

Discussion

I think what she expressed with her annoyance was that she considered the sessions important and particularly at this time she could not do without them. She felt free to express her anger, thus indicating that her fear of loss and her feelings of guilt were no longer overwhelming. I asked myself at the same time why I had not hurried more and ended a preceding meeting earlier to try to get to the session on time. It seemed to me that I had made Mrs. K. wait, as if I wanted to delay something, which was difficult for me as well and which I did not want to fully realise. With her accusation as to whether I could imagine what this situation meant for her, she had brought me back to reality. Yet in her defiantly presented message that she had had a good weekend, there was less resentment and bitterness as she could let me know by the end of the session that she was sad to leave.

Maybe I had conducted myself more like an MOT mechanic, who lets the customers wait and does his routine investigations without considering the customer's personal feelings, just like a sort of super-ego agency, which awards a seal of approval and thus the job is done. In contrast, she had reminded me in the previous session how difficult it was for her to leave and that she wondered whether this touched me personally as well, which had made her sad and embarrassed. She had then gone on to talk about her plans to grow fruit and vegetables and her hope for a good harvest, which, I believe, was a rather clear expression of her gratitude. At the same time, she had realised that the feelings about ending the joint work were different for students and lecturers, because of, I think, the unequal distribution of dependency.

The two last sessions

Her opening comment in the *penultimate session* was that it 'was peculiar to know' that this was her penultimate session. She was very conscious of this fact. She added that there were 'dreams in a waiting queue', which she had noticed when she had not been able to go to sleep immediately. She described these dreams as 'raw material which has not yet been fully formed' to allow access to her 'internal pictures'.

She continued that last night there had been a 'thunderstorm' and when she went back to sleep afterwards, she had dreamed of her father, who was significantly younger, maybe 60 or 70 years old. He worked as an adviser in an impressive building and had two assistants to support him. She was pleased and surprised that she had access to him and the two assistants asked her many questions.

I interpreted that the 'thunderstorm' was an expression of the violence and ferocity of her feelings about the imminent separation. I added that the father, my age approximately, with his assistants in an impressive building, might be a reminder of the loss of her father in the early part of her analysis and at the same time express a wish not to lose access to me as an 'adviser'.

She said that she wondered whether this was just 'wishful thinking' or a consoling 'sticking plaster' on my part. This was not clear to her.

By the close of the session, she seemed to be very preoccupied with her feelings and thoughts.

I, too, began to reflect further about her comment and her dream and put the supposition to her that the 'thunderstorm' and the rolling thunder as well as the dreams in the 'waiting queue' could be an expression of her anger about me having made her wait the day before.

She seemed sceptical, as she had been frequently before when I had addressed her anger. But as the session came to an end, there was no time to elaborate on these ideas.

In the *last session*, she said that she had wanted to be 'brave', but she had known that she would cry today when she saw me. And then she cried.

After a pause, she told me that she had been to the MOT today. The mechanic had been friendly to her and not severe as she had expected and he had declared her car safe. She could continue to drive it.

After a short pause, still sad, she told me about a film, *Orpheus in the Underworld*, which she had seen on TV the night before. She described how the ferry man had helped Orpheus to cross the river Styx to get to the realm of the dead, how he managed to placate the hellhound Cerberus, but then could not resist the temptation to turn around to look at his wife Eurydice and so lost her forever. In this moment, he was overwhelmed by sadness and guilt as he knew that there was no going back.

These thoughts had gone through her head as she had visited her mother's grave that morning to breathe a bit of fresh spring air while going for a walk before the session.

I was touched by the imagery she brought. It seemed to be self-explanatory and I did not have the feeling that I needed to comment except that *she*, too, had said that she would be very sad when she *saw* me for the last time today.

She then let me know that the gardener who looked after the plot of land she had leased had phoned her. She would take his advice and go to the place on the weekend as the first few things such as radishes and lettuce had already grown and were ready to be harvested.

I indicated that I thought there was a link between the three images of the friendly MOT mechanic, of Orpheus who looks back to recognise his loss with sadness and guilt and the call from the gardener to tell her that there was new growth.

She said she noticed how much had changed and how quickly time passed. She thought of her hallucinations at the beginning of her analysis, which in the course of time had changed into 'dreams', which gave her a feeling of 'satiation'. She remembered the image of the nutshell bobbing aimlessly in a 'sea of timelessness', and now thought this sea had changed into a river, which forced her into a given direction. But now this movement could no longer be halted.

She cried as she left the session saying good-bye to me.

Discussion

I think the last two sessions illustrate Mrs. K.'s psychic development in a condensed form. The 'thunderstorm' and the rolling thunder after the session in which I had made her wait for me had not developed into a psychotic storm as it would have at the beginning of treatment. Instead, they provided the 'raw material of dreams', as she put it, as in the dream where she met her father as 'an adviser in an impressive building'. I think that she expressed a wish not to lose me as an 'adviser', even though she had to leave.

The friendly MOT mechanic passing her car indicated that her super-ego had developed from a persecutory into a supportive authority, expressing confidence and helping her check reality, like the ferryman Charon who had taken Orpheus across without waking the hellhound. However, the look back made it painfully conscious that there was no way back and she had to accept a loss.

She had done this by visiting her mother's grave before coming to the last session to breathe a bit of fresh spring air and to give her an appetite for new life. The gardener had phoned her to tell her that things had already grown and would be ready for harvesting. And I think in this way, she fairly directly expressed her gratitude to me.

Just as she could harvest the fruit of her labour, something had grown inside her. The hallucinations of the beginning of her analysis had turned into dreams, which 'nourished' her, and by bringing her dreams to the sessions, and thus allowing me to access and understand her internal world, she had likewise fed and 'nourished' me.

Admittedly, her gratitude was linked to the painful feeling of the passing of time and the two of us being separated now. Nothing could be reversed once it was taken out of the 'sea of timelessness' and put into the river, whose course has a direction and whose current pulls one along continuously.

This thought made her very sad once again at the end of the session, for now, she knew, she had to say the final good-bye.

Gratitude, reparation and transience

I think that, during her last treatment sessions, Mrs. K. did not only express her gratitude, but also demonstrated her increased capacity for reparation. Despite feeling disappointed by me at times and angered by my lateness in the third last session before the ending, she was able to forgive me and did not retreat into feelings of resentment. Likewise, she was not hindered by overwhelming feelings of guilt in voicing her criticism and her doubts openly to me.

She expressed the thought that my comment that she wished to keep me as an 'adviser' could be seen as a kind of 'wishful thinking' or a 'sticking plaster' to make the parting easier for her as well as for me. Presumably, she had picked up on what I did not want to admit to myself so readily, namely that I felt relief about the ending of our work as well and wanted to bring it to a good conclusion, just as the lecturer wants her students to get a good degree. In this way, she was right in suspecting that the lecturer *did not have the same* experience towards her students as they had towards her. Nevertheless, she could admit somewhat embarrassed that she had hoped that the ending would touch me as well and that I would not just replace her with the next 'customer', as in the MOT.

I think that this change reflects an acknowledgement of dependency and difference, which, as I have described, I regard as the prerequisite of the experience of gratitude. Of course, I, too, was affected by the ending, but not in the *same way* as her. For Mrs. K., the end of the analysis meant relinquishing a security that had become part of her life, while I and my colleagues could continue as 'advisers' in an 'impressive building'.

In the introduction, I have described gratitude as a feeling which does not only require the overcoming of envy, anger and endless self-accusations by activating processes of reparation, but also establishes *a reciprocal relationship* in which the giver (in the sense of 'reciprocal benevolence') is also the recipient.

However, this reciprocity is never symmetrical. It is probably one of the painful aspects of the analytic relationship, and maybe of all human experience in general, that it is and remains *asymmetrical*. Only through the acknowledgement of this asymmetry is it possible to accept other painful aspects of reality, such as the limitations as to what can be done in a treatment, or the fact that all good experiences are finite. However, just as all good experiences are finite, we can add *that the bad experiences cannot go on endlessly either.* [4]

In this way, gratitude is closely linked to our readiness to relinquish control over our objects. In Mrs. K., this capacity had grown over a long period of time, and she was able to gradually leave the time-lessness of the 'realm of the dead' and began to feel less terrorised by the 'hellhound' of a psychotic super-ego organisation. But it was painful for her to take this last step at the end of treatment. She knew she was going to cry when she saw me the last time, but, like Orpheus, she had to face this reality and return to her own life.

It seems significant to me that the experience of parting is so often communicated by the gaze (see Chapter 2). Maybe we should have a closer look at what is expressed by the gaze in the moment of parting. It is the experience of being seen which can mean acceptance, rejection, criticism, gratitude or sadness and it is the gaze of the analyst which the patient takes with them from the consulting room into their outside lives. But this is probably a subject which requires further exploration (see Steiner 2014).

I just want to indicate here that the feeling of gratitude is probably fed by various sources. One of these is the capacity to take in something good, which means overcoming feelings of envy, grievance and shame. A second one, and possibly a more important one, is presumably the capacity for reparation, enabling us to forgive but conversely to have the experience of being forgiven (see Rey 1986). A third one might be the capacity to acknowledge the transience and limitation of all human endeavour and not to close one's eyes to the painful fact that all good experiences are finite. Revenge and retaliation give the illusion of endlessness, as if life could go on forever. In contrast,

Seneca already reminded us of the transitoriness of life in his book about rage pointing out that 'our short-lived troubles' will soon come to an end when we look back and realise that 'death will be upon us' (Seneca 1928, 'On Anger', Book III, 43).

Notes

1 'Let us give the mind that peace which is given by constant meditation upon wholesome maxims, by good actions, and by a mind directed to the pursuit of honour alone. Let us set our own conscience fully at rest, but make no efforts to gain credit for ourselves: so long as we deserve well, let us be satisfied, even if we should be ill spoken of' (Seneca 1928, 'On Anger', Book III, 41).
2 A related topic, which cannot be dealt with here in detail, is the relationship between gratitude and sacrifice (see Eliade 1978).
3 This idea I owe to John Steiner, who takes the view that gratitude can only set in after reparation. 'Gratitude is no motivation for reparation. The motivation for reparation is guilt and can only set in when the hatred of the object has been made conscious' (personal communication 2015).
4 Personal communication, Hanna Segal (2008).

Bibliography

Abraham, K. (1913). Restitutions and transformations of scopophilia in psychoneurotics, 169–234. In: Abraham, K. (1968). *Selected Papers on Psycho-Analysis* (7th Impression). London: Hogarth Press.

Abraham, K. (1919). A particular form of neurotic resistance against the psycho-analytic method, 303–311. *Selected Papers of Karl Abraham*. London: Hogarth Press.

Abraham, K. (1924). A short study of the development of the libido, viewed in the light of mental disorders, 418–501. *Selected Papers of Karl Abraham*. London: Hogarth Press.

Amati, S. (1987). Some thoughts on torture. *Free Associations*, 1(8), 94–114.

Andreae, J. V. (1619). (1975 Edition). *Christianopolis*. Stuttgart: Reclam.

Arlow, J. A. (1984). Disturbances of the sense of time – with special reference to the experience of timelessness. *Psychoanal. Q.*, 53(1), 13–37.

Arlow, J. A. (1986). Psychoanalysis and time. *J. Am. Psychoanal. Assoc.*, 34(3), 507–528.

Assmann, A. (2016). *Formen des Vergessens*. Göttingen: Wallstein.

Auerhahn, N. C. & Laub, D. (1984). Annihilation and restoration: post-traumatic memory as pathway and obstacle to recovery. *Int. Rev. Psycho-Anal.*, 11(3), 327–344.

Bacon, F. (1627). *Nova Atlantis*. London.

Balint, M. (1968). *The Basic Fault: Therapeutic Aspects of Regression*. London: Tavistock Publications.

Balint, M. (1969). Trauma and object relationship. *Int. J. Psycho-Anal.*, 50(4), 429–435.

Baranger, M., Baranger, W. & Mom, J. M. (1988). The infantile psychic trauma from us to Freud: pure trauma, retroactivity and retroaction. *Int. J. Psycho-Anal.*, 69(1), 113–128.

Baranger, M. & Baranger, W. (2008). The analytic situation as a dynamic field. *Int. J. Psycho-Anal.*, 89(4), 795–826.

Barzilai, M. (2007). Melancholia as world history: W. G. Sebald's rewriting of Hegel in Die Ringe des Saturn, 73–89. In: Fuchs, A. & Long, J. J. (Eds.).

(2007). *W. G. Sebald and the Writing of History.* Würzburg: Königshausen & Neumann.

Bell, D. (2006). Existence in time: development or catastrophe. *Pschoanal. Q.*, 75(3), 783–805.

Bergson, H. (1907). *L'Évolution Créatrice.* Paris: Alcan.

Bick, E. (1968). The experience of the skin in early object-relations. *Int. J. Psycho-Anal.*, 49(2–3), 484–486.

Bick, E. (1986). Further considerations on the function of the skin in early object-relations. *Brit. J. Psychoanal.*, 2(4), 292–299.

Bion, W. R. (1959). Attacks on linking. *Int. J. Psycho-Anal.*, 40(5–6), 308–315.

Bion, W. R. (1961). *Experiences in Groups and Other Papers.* London: Tavistock Publications.

Bion, W. R. (1962). *Learning from Experience.* London: Heinemann.

Birksted-Breen, D. (2003). Time and the après-coup. *Int. J. Psycho-Anal.*, 84(6), 1501–1515.

Blass, R. (2015). Conceptualizing splitting: on the different meanings of splitting and their implications for the understanding of the person and the analytic process. *Int. J. Psycho-Anal.*, 96(1), 123–139.

Bohleber, W. (2000). Die Entwicklung der Traumatheorie in der Psychoanalyse. *Psyche – Z. Psychonal.*, 54, 797–839.

Bohleber, W. (2007). Remembrance, trauma and collective memory: a battle for memory in psychoanalysis. *Int. J. Psycho-Anal.*, 88(2), 329–352.

Bohleber, W. (2010). *Destructiveness, Intersubjectivity and Trauma: The Identity Crisis of Modern Psychoanalysis*, 35–57. London: Karnac.

Bohleber, W. (2017). Zur Geschichte und Konzeptualisierung des Traumabegriffs in der Psychoanalyse. In: Horn, E. & Weiss, H. (Eds.). (2017). *Trauma und unbewusste Phantasie.* Frankfurt: Brandes & Apsel.

Bollnow, O. F.(1954). Über die Dankbarkeit. *Die Sammlung*, 9, 169–177.

Brenman, E. (1985). Cruelty and narrowmindedness. *Int. J. Psycho-Anal.*, 66(3), 273–281.

Brenman, E. (2006). *Recovery of the Lost Good Object.* London, New York: Routledge.

Brenman Pick, I. (1985). Working through in the countertransference. *Int. J. Psycho-Anal.*, 66(2), 157–166.

Brenman Pick, I. (1993). Zorn – eine der sieben Todsünden. Zur Arbeitsweise des Gewissens in Individuum und Gesellschaft, 84–99. In: Gutwinski-Jeggle, J. & Rotmann, J. M. (Eds.). (1993). *Die klugen Sinne pflegend: Psychoanalytische und kulturkritische Beiträge: Hermann Beland zu Ehren*, Tübingen: Edition Diskord.

Brenner, I. (2001). *Dissociation of Trauma: Theory, Phenomenology, and Technique.* Madison: International Universities Press.

Brenner, I. (2014). *Dark Matters: Exploring the Realm of Psychic Devastation.* London: Karnac.

Britton, R. (1989). The missing link: parental sexuality in the Oedipus complex, 83–101. In: Britton, R., Feldman, M., O'Shaughnessy, E. & Steiner, J. (Eds.). (1989). *The Oedipus Complex Today: Clinical Implications.* London: Karnac.

Britton, R. (1998). Weitere Überlegungen zur dritten Position, 97–120. In: Britton, R., Feldman, M. & Steiner, J.; Weiss, H. & Frank, C. (Eds.). (1998). *Narzissmus, Allmacht und psychische Realität: Beiträge der Westlodge-Konferenz III*. Tübingen: Edition Diskord.

Britton, R. (2003). Emancipation from the Superego, 103–116. In: Britton, R. (2003). *Sex, Death and the Superego: Experiences in Psychoanalysis*. London: Karnac.

Britton, R. (2005). Endogeneous trauma and psycho-phobia. *Bull. Brit. Psychoanal. Soc.*, 41(3), 5–16.

Bronstein, C. (2016). Delusion and reparation: the analysis of a psychotic adolescent. *Bull. Brit. Psychoanal. Soc.*, 52(2), 2–13.

Broucek, F. J. (1982). Shame and its relationship to early narcissistic developments. *Int. J. Psycho-Anal.*, 63(3), 369–378.

Brown, L. (2005). The cognitive effects of trauma: the reversal of alpha function and the formation of a beta screen. *Psychoanal. Q.*, 74(2), 397–420.

Brown, L. (2006). Julie's museum: the evolution of thinking, dreaming and historicization in the treatment of traumatized patients. *Int. J. Psycho-Anal.*, 87(6), 1569–1585.

Campanella, T. (1623). Civitas solis: Idea rei publicae philosophicae, 115–169. In: Heinisch, K.-J. (Ed.). (1960). *Der utopische Staat*. Reinbek: Rowohlt.

Coates, S. W. & Moore, M. S. (1997). The complexity of early trauma: representation and transformation. *Psychoanal. Inquiry*, 17(3), 286–311.

Colarusso, C. A. (1979). The development of time sense – from birth to object constancy. *Int. J. Psycho-Anal.*, 60(2), 243–251.

De Masi, F. (1989). The superego. *Rivista di Psicoanalsi*, 35, 390–430.

De Masi, F. (1997). Intimidation at the helm: superego and hallucinosis in the analytic treatment of a psychosis. *Int. J. Psycho-Anal.*, 78(3), 561–576.

De Masi, F. (2015). *Working with Difficult Patients: From Neurosis to Psychosis*. London: Karnac.

De Masi, F. (2017). Über die Auswirkungen emotionaler Traumatisierung – Arbeiten mit schwierigen Patienten, 90–103. In: Horn, E. & Weiss, H. (Eds.). (2017). *Trauma und unbewusste Phantasie*. Frankfurt: Brandes & Apsel.

Demmerling, C. & Landweer, H. (2007). *Philosophie der Gefühle: Von Achtung bis Zorn*. Stuttgart/Weimar: J. B. Metzler.

Deutsch, H. (1934). Über einen Typus mit Pseudoaffektivität ('Als ob'). *Int. Z. Psychoanal.*, 20, 323–335.

Ducasse, D., Courtet, P. & Olié, E. (2014). Physical and social pains in borderline disorder and neuroanatomical correlates: a systematic review. *Curr. Psychiatry Rep.*, 16(5), 1–12.

Eco, U. (2013). *The Book of Legendary Lands*. London: Rizzoli.

Eickhoff, F.-W. (2005). Über Nachträglichkeit: Die Modernität eines alten Konzepts. *Jahrb. Psychoanal.*, 51, 139–161.

Eisler, J. (1919). Ein Fall von krankhafter 'Schamsucht'. *Int. Zschr. f. Psychoanal.*, 5(3), 193–199.

Erikson, E. H. (1959). *Identity and the Life Cycle*. New York: International Universities Press.

Erpenbeck, J. (2006). *The Old Child*. London: Portobello Books.

Erpenbeck, J. (2011). *Visitation*. London: Portobello Books.

Erpenbeck, J. (2015). *The End of Days*. London: Portobello Books.

Feldman, M. (1997). Projective identification: the analyst's involvement. *Int. J. Psycho-Anal.*, 78(2), 227–241.

Feldman, M. (2008). Grievance: the underlying oedipal configuration. *Int. J. Psycho-Anal.*, 89(4), 743–758.

Fenichel, O. (1937). The scopophilic instinct and identification. *Int. J. Psycho-Anal.*, 18, 6–34.

Fenichel, O. (1945). The concept of trauma in contemporary psycho-analytical theory. *Int. J. Psycho-Anal.*, 26, 33–44.

Ferenczi, S. (1931). Child-analysis in the analysis of adults. *Int. J. Psycho-Anal.*, 12, 468–482.

Ferenczi, S. (1949). Confusion of tongues between adults and the child: the language of tenderness and of passion. *Int. J. Psycho-Anal.*, 30, 225–230.

Fonagy, P. (2001). *Attachment Theory and Psychoanalysis*. London, New York: Routledge.

Fonagy, P. & Target, M. (2001). Mit der Realität spielen. Zur Doppelgesichtigkeit psychischer Realität von Borderline-Patienten. *Psyche – Z. Psychoanal.*, 55, 961–995.

Fonagy, P., Gergely, G., Jurist, E. L. & Target, M. (2002). *Affect Regulation, Mentalization and the Development of the Self*. New York: Other Press.

Fonagy, P., Target, M., Gergely, G., Allen, J. G. & Bateman, A. W. (2003). The developmental roots of borderline personality disorder in early attachment relationships: a theory and some evidence. *Psychoanal. Inq.*, 23(3), 412–459.

Frank, C. (2002). Mains tenant le vide – Maintenant le vide: Überlegungen zu Giacomettis Skulpturen (von ca. 1947 bis ca. 1952) und zum analytischen Prozess. *Jahrb. Psychoanal.*, 44, 63–104.

Frank, C. (2003a). Eine mögliche 'Abweichung der normalen Gegenübertragung': Entgrenzung als Misskonzeption der analytischen Beziehung, 97–124. In: Frank, C. & Weiss, H. (Eds.). (2003), *Normale Gegenübertragung und mögliche Abweichungen: Zur Aktualität von R. Money-Kyrles Verständnis des Gegenübertragungsprozesses*. Tübingen: Edition Diskord.

Frank, C. (2003b). 'Ver-rückt': Realisieren perverser Momente in der Übertragung und Gegenübertragung. *Jahrb. Psychoanal.*, 46, 91–113.

Frank, C. (2006). Giorgio Morandis 'Natura Morta': Überlegungen zum Interaktionsprozess. *Psyche – Z. Psychoanal.*, 60(6), 491–514.

Frank, C. (2009). *Melanie Klein in Berlin: Her First Psychoanalyses of Children*. London, New York: Routledge.

Frank, C. (2012). Wiedergutmachung – Zur Entstehung eines neuen Konzepts aus Melanie Kleins ersten kinderanalytischen Erfahrungen. *Jahrb. Psychoanal.*, 65, 81–106.

Frank, C. (2013). Wenn 'Ordnung wichtiger wird als das Leben' – welche Konzepte helfen uns in der Gegenübertragung?, 415–421. In: Walker, C. E., Blaß, H., Johne, M. & Paul, R. (Eds.). (2013). *Psychoanalytisches Arbeiten – innerer und äußerer Rahmen*. *Tagungsband, Herbsttagung der Deutschen Psychoanalytischen Vereinigung*. Gießen: Psychosozial Verlag.

Frank, C. (2015a). Wenn Blicke vernichten können – Zur Theorie und Klinik von Raum und Zeit angreifenden Über-Ich-Organisationen, 133–153. In: Frank, C., Kidess, A. (Eds.). (2015). *Zur Psychoanalyse im Hier und Jetzt*. Frankfurt: Brandes & Apsel.

Frank, C. (2015b). Zum Wurzeln der Symbolisierung in 'sinnhaften' unbewussten Phantasien körperlicher Erfahrungen – Der kleinianische Symbolisierungsbegriff. *Jahrb. Psychoanal.*, 71, 41–63.

Frank, C. (2015c). 'If I can choose' – zur psychoanalytischen Orientierungsarbeit. Lecture at the Congress 'On Gratitude' in honour of Edna O'Shaughnessy's 90th birthday, Stuttgart.

Frank, C. (2017). Zur Erforschung der Bedeutung von Symbolisierungsprozessen in der Auseinandersetzung mit Kunstwerken am Beispiel einiger Stilllebenvariationen Giorgio Morandis, 69–96. In: Weiss, H. & Rumpeltes, R. (Eds.). (2017). *Hanna Segal Revisited: Zur Aktualität ihres Werkes*. Frankfurt: Brandes & Apsel.

Frank, C. & Weiss, H. (Eds.). (2003). *Normale Gegenübertragung und mögliche Abweichungen. Zur Aktualität von R. Money-Kyrles Verständnis des Gegenübertragungskonzeptes*. Tübingen: Edition Diskord.

Frank, C. & Weiss, H. (Eds.). (2007). *Projektive Identifizierung. Ein Schlüsselkonzept der psychoanalytischen Therapie*. Stuttgart: Klett-Cotta.

Freud, S. (1896a). Heredity and the aetiology of neurosis. *Standard Edition Volume 3*, 143–156.

Freud, S. (1896b). Further remarks on the neuro-psychoses of defence. *Standard Edition Volume 3*, 162–185.

Freud, S. (1899a). Screen memories. *Standard Edition Volume 3*, 37–56.

Freud, S. (1905d). Three essays on the theory of sexuality. *Standard Edition Volume 7*, 135–243.

Freud, S. (1909b). Analysis of a phobia of a five-year-old boy. *Standard Edition Volume 10*, 5–147.

Freud, S. (1909d). Notes on a case of obsessional neurosis. *Standard Edition Volume 10*, 155–249.

Freud, S. (1911c). Psycho-analytic notes on an autobiographical account of paranoia (dementia paranoids). *Standard Edition Volume 12*, 9–79.

Freud, S. (1914g). Remembering, repeating and working-through (further recommendations on the technique of psycho-analysis II). *Standard Edition Volume 12*, 147–156.

Freud, S. (1916d). Some character-types with in psycho-analytic work. *Standard Edition Volume 14*, 311–333.

Freud, S. (1916–17a). Introductory lectures. *Standard Edition Volumes 15–16*.

Freud, S. (1916–17g). Mourning and melancholia. *Standard Edition Volume 14*, 243–258.

Freud, S. (1918b). From the history of an infantile neurosis. *Standard Edition Volume 17*, 7–122.

Freud, S. (1920g). Beyond the pleasure principle. *Standard Edition Volume 18*, 7–64.

Freud, S. (1923b). The ego and the id. *Standard Edition Volume 19*, 12–59.

Freud, S. (1924b). Neurosis and psychosis. *Standard Edition Volume 19*, 149–153.

Freud, S. (1924c). The economic problem of masochism. *Standard Edition Volume 19*, 159–170.

Freud, S. (1924e). The loss of reality in neurosis and psychosis. *Standard Edition Volume 19*, 183–187.

Freud, S. (1925a). A note on the 'mystic writing-pad'. *Standard Edition Volume 19*, 227–232.

Freud, S. (1925h). Negation. *Standard Edition Volume 19*, 235–239.

Freud, S. (1926d). Inhibitions, symptoms and anxiety. *Standard Edition Volume 30*, 87–172.

Freud, S. (1927e). Fetishism. *Standard Edition Volume 21*, 152–157.

Freud, S. (1937c). Analysis terminable and interminable. *Standard Edition Volume 23*, 216–253.

Freud, S. (1937d). Constructions in analysis. *Standard Edition Volume 23*, 255–270.

Freud, S. (1940e). Splitting of the ego in neurosis and psychosis. *Standard Edition Volume 23*, 275–283.

Freud, S. (1942a). Psychopathic characters on the stage. *Standard Edition Volume 7*, 305–310.

Freud, S. (1950a). *The Complete Letters of Sigmund Freud to Wilhelm Fliess.* (Masson, J. M., Ed. 1985). Cambridge MA: Harvard Universities Press.

Freud, S. & Breuer, J. (1895d). *Studies on Hysteria. Standard Edition of the Complete Psychological Works of Sigmund Freud, Volume 2.*

Friedjung, J. K. (1913). Über verschiedene Quellen kindlicher Schamhaftigkeit. *Int. Zschr. f. Psychoanal.*, 1, 362–364.

Fuchs, A. & Long, J. J. (Eds.). (2007). *W. G. Sebald and the Writing of History.* Würzburg: Königshausen & Neumann.

Gabbard, G. O. (1995). Countertransference: the emerging common ground. *Int. J. Psycho-Anal.*, 76(3), 475–485.

Gabbard, G. O., Miller, L. A. & Martinez, M. (2006). A neurobiological perspective on mentalizing and internal object relations in traumatized patients with borderline personality disorder, 123–140. In: Allen, G. & Fonagy, P. (Eds.). (2006). *The Handbook of Mentalization-Based Treatment.* London: Wiley.

Garland, C. (Ed.). (1998). *Understanding Trauma: A Psychoanalytical Approach.* London, New York: Karnac.

Gergely, G. & Watson, J. S. (1996). The social biofeedback model of parental mirroring. *Int. J. Psycho-Anal.*, 77(6), 1181–1212.

Giovacchini, P. L. (1967). The frozen object. *Int. J. Psycho-Anal.*, 48, 61–67.

Giovacchini, P. L. (1993). The concrete patient, massive trauma and the psychosomatic focus, 103–127. In: Giovacchini, P. L. (1993). *Borderline Patients, the Psychosomatic Focus, and the Therapeutic Process*. Northvale, New Jersey: Jason Aronson.

Goldberg, C. (1991). *Understanding Shame*. Northvale, New Jersey: Jason Aronson.

Gomperz, T. (Ed.). (1864). *Philodemos: De Ira Liber*. Leipzig: Teubner.

Green, A. (1983). The dead mother, 142–173. In: Green, A. (1986). *On Private Madness*. London: Hogarth.

Grinberg, L. (1962). On a specific aspect of countertransference due to the patient's projective identification. *Int. J. Psycho-Anal.*, 43, 436–440.

Grinberg, L. (1968). On acting out and its role in the psychoanalytic process. *Int. J. Psycho-Anal.*, 49(2–3), 171–178.

Grubrich-Simitis, I. (1979). Extremtraumatisierung als kumulatives Trauma: Psychoanalytische Studien über seelische Nachwirkungen der Konzentrationslagerhaft bei Überlebenden und ihren Kindern. *Psyche – Z. Psychoanal.*, 33, 991–1023.

Grunberger, B. (1971). *Le Narcissisme: Essais de Psychanalyse*. Paris: Payot.

Gutwinski-Jeggle, J. (1992). Trauma und Zeiterleben: Theoretische Überlegungen. *Jahrb. Psychoanal.*, 29, 167–214.

Hall, J. (1605). (1937 Edition). *Mundus alter et idem, sive terra australis ante hac semper incognita longis itineribus peregrine academici nuperrime lustra*. Cambridge MA: Harvard Universities Press.

Hartocollis, P. (1978). Time and affect in borderline disorders. *Int. J. Psycho-Anal.*, 59(2–3), 157–163.

Hartocollis, P. (1983). *Time and Timelessness*. New York: International Universities Press.

Haubl, R. (2001). Der böse Blick, 67–72. In: Haubl, J. (Ed.). (2009). *Neidisch sind immer nur die anderen: Über die Unfähigkeit, zufrieden zu sein*. München: C. H. Beck.

Hegel, G. W. F. (1807). (2018 Edition). *The Phenomenology of Spirit*. Oxford: Oxford University Press.

Hegel, G. W. F. (1830). (1971 Edition). *Encyclopaedia of the Philosophical Sciences, Part 2 and 3*. Oxford: Clarendon Press.

Heidegger, M. (1927). (1962 Edition). *Being and Time*. Oxford: Blackwell Publishers.

Held, T. (2014). Child Survivors der Nazi-Verfolgung: was haben wir damals verstanden und was nicht? *Psyche – Z. Psychoanal.*, 68, 681–703.

Henningsen, F. (2000). Destruktion und Schuld. Spaltungen und Reintegrationsprozesse in der Analyse eines traumatisierten Patienten. *Psyche – Z. Psychoanal.*, 54, 974–1001.

Henningsen, F. (2008). Konkretistische Fusion, Agieren und Symbolisieren bei schwerer frühkindlicher Traumatisierung. *Psyche – Z. Psychoanal.*, 62, 1148–1169.

Henningsen, F. (2012). *Psychoanalyse mit traumatisierten Patienten*. Stuttgart: Klett-Cotta.

Hollan, D. (2012). Cultures and their discontents: on the cultural mediation of shame and guilt. *Psychoanal. Inq.*, 32(6), 570–581.

Horn, E. (2015). Aspekte einer inneren Sektenorganisation, 107–131. In: Frank, C. & Kidess, A. (Eds.). (2015). *Zur Psychoanalyse des Hier und Jetzt*. Frankfurt: Brandes & Apsel.

Horn, E. & Weiss, H. (2010). Der Nebel – Unsichtbarkeit als Schutz und als Abwehrorganisation. *Psyche – Z. Psychoanal.*, 64, 236–257.

Hühn, H. (2004). Zorn, 1386–1390. In: Ritter, H., Gründer, K. & Gabriel, G. (2004). *Historisches Wörterbuch der Philosophie, Bd. 12*. Basel: Schwabe.

Isaacs, S. (1948). The nature and function of phantasy. *Int. J. Psycho-Anal.*, 29, 73–97.

Jacobs, T. J. (1986). On countertransference enactments. *J. Am. Psychoanal. Assoc.*, 34(2), 289–307.

Jacobs, T. J. (1993). The inner experiences of the psychoanalyst: their contribution to the analytic process. *Int. J. Psycho-Anal.*, 74(1), 7–14.

Jahn, O. (1855). *Über den Aberglauben des bösen Blicks bei den Alten*, 28–110. Leipzig: S. Hirzel Verlag.

Janin, C. (2007). *La honte, ses figures et ses destins*. Paris: Presses Universitaires de France.

Janin, C. (2015). Shame, hatred and pornography: variations on an aspect of current times. *Int. J. Psycho-Anal.*, 96(6), 1603–1614.

Joseph, B. (1971). A clinical contribution to the analysis of a perversion. *Int. J. Psycho-Anal.*, 52(4), 441–449.

Joseph, B. (1975). The patient who is difficult to reach, 205–216. In: Giovacchini, P. L. (Ed.). (1975). *Tactics and Techniques in Psychoanalytic Therapy, Vol. 2: Countertransference*. New York: Jason Aronson.

Joseph, B. (1982). Addiction to near-death. *Int. J. Psycho-Anal.*, 63(4), 449–456.

Joseph, B. (1985). Transference: the total situation. *Int. J. Psycho-Anal.*, 66(4), 447–454.

Joseph, B. (1989). *Psychic Equilibrium and Psychic Change: Selected Papers of Betty Joseph*. (Eds. Feldman, M., Bott Spillius, E.) London, New York: Routledge.

Katan, M. (1959). Schreber's hereafter: its building-up (Aufbau) and its downfall. *Psychoanal. St. Child*. 14, 314–382.

Keilson, H. (1979). (2005 Edition). *Sequentielle Traumatisierung bei Kindern: Untersuchungen zum Schicksal jüdischer Kriegswaisen*. Gießen: Psychosozial-Verlag.

Kernberg, O. F. (2004). *Aggressivity, Narcissism, and Self-Destructiveness in the Psychoanalytic Relationship*. New Haven: Yale University Press.

Kestenberg, J. S. (1980). Psychoanalyses of children of survivors from the Holocaust: case presentations and assessment. *J. Am. Psychoanal. Assoc.*, 28(4), 775–804.

Khan, M. M. (1964). Ego distortion, cumulative trauma, and the role of reconstruction in the analytic situation. *Int. J. Psycho-Anal.*, 45, 272–279.

Kinston, W. & Cohen, J. (1986). Primal repression: clinical and theoretical aspects. *Int. J. Psycho-Anal.*, 67(3), 235–242.

Klein, M. (1929). (1975 Edition). Early anxiety situations reflected in a work of art and the creative impulse, 210–218. *The Collected Writings of Melanie Klein, Vol. 1.* London: Hogarth Press.

Klein, M. (1930). (1975 Edition). The importance of symbol-formation in the development of the ego, 219–232. *The Collected Writings of Melanie Klein, Vol. 1.* London: Hogarth Press.

Klein, M. (1932). (1975 Edition). *The Psycho-Analysis of Children: The Collected Writings of Melanie Klein, Vol. 2.* London: Hogarth Press.

Klein, M. (1935). (1975 Edition). Contribution to the psychogenesis of manic-depressive states, 262–289. *The Collected Writings of Melanie Klein, Vol. 1.* London: Hogarth Press.

Klein, M. (1936). Lectures on Technique, 25–94. In: Steiner, J. (Ed.). (2017). *Lectures on Technique by Melanie Klein.* London, New York: Routledge.

Klein, M. (1937). (1975 Edition). Love, guilt and reparation, 306–343. *The Collected Writings of Melanie Klein, Vol. 1.* London: Hogarth Press.

Klein, M. (1940). (1975 Edition). Mourning and its relation to manic-depressive states, 344–369. *The Collected Writings of Melanie Klein, Vol. 1.* London: Hogarth Press.

Klein, M. (1946). (1975 Edition). Notes on some schizoid mechanisms, 1–24. *The Collected Writings of Melanie Klein, Vol. 3.* London: Hogarth Press.

Klein, M. (1948). (1975 Edition). On the theory of anxiety and guilt, 25–42. *The Collected Writings of Melanie Klein, Vol. 3.* London: Hogarth Press.

Klein, M. (1950). (1975 Edition). On the criteria for the termination of a psycho-analysis, 43–47. *The Collected Writings of Melanie Klein, Vol. 3.* London: Hogarth Press.

Klein, M. (1957). (1975 Edition). Envy and gratitude, 176–235. *The Collected Writings of Melanie Klein, Vol. 3.* London: Hogarth Press.

Klein, M. (1958). (1975 Edition). On the development of mental functioning, 236–246. *The Collected Writings of Melanie Klein, Vol. 3.* London: Hogarth Press.

Klein, M., (1963). (1975 Edition). On the sense of loneliness, 300–317. *The Collected Writings of Melanie Klein, Vol. 3.* London: Hogarth Press.

Klein, M. & Rivière, J. (1937). *Love, Hate and Reparation.* London: Hogarth Press.

Kleist, H. v. (1810). (2005 Edition). *Michael Kohlhaas.* Brooklyn, London: Melville House.

Kogan, I. (2007). *The Struggle Against Mourning.* New York: Jason Aronson.

Kohut, H. (1966). Forms and transformations of narcissism. *J. Am. Psychoanal. Assoc.*, 14(2), 242–272.

Kohut, H. (1968). *The Analysis of the Self: A Systematic Approach to the Psychoanalytic Treatment of Narcissistic Personality Disorders.* New York: International Universities Press.

Krystal, H. (2000). Psychische Widerständigkeit: Anpassung und Restitution bei Holocaust-Überlebenden. *Psyche – Z. Psychoanal.*, 54, 840–859.

Küchenhoff, J. (2007). Sehen und Gesehenwerden: Identität und Beziehung im Blick. *Psyche – Z. Psychoanal.*, 61(5), 445–462.

Küchenhoff, J., Pfeiffer, J. & Pietzcker, C. (2013). *Scham. Freiburger literaturpsychologische Gespräche, Bd. 32.* Würzburg: Königshausen & Neumann.

Lacan, J. (1949). The mirror stage as formative of the function of the I as revealed in psychoanalytic experience, 75–81. In: Lacan, J. (2006). *Écrits.* New York: W. W. Norton.

Lang, H. (1978). Geschichtlichkeit des Daseins oder Entwicklung des Soma? Überlegungen zum wissenschaftlichen Standort der Psychoanalyse, 121–138. In: Kraus, A. (Ed.). (1978). *Leib, Geist, Geschichte: Brennpunkte anthropologischer Psychiatrie.* Heidelberg: Hüthig.

Lansky, M. R. (1994). Shame: contemporary psychoanalytic perspectives. *J. Amer. Acad. Psychoanal.*, 22(3), 433–441.

Lansky, M. R. (2001). Hidden shame, working through, and the problem of forgiveness in The Tempest. *J. Am. Psychoanal. Assoc.*, 49(3), 1005–1033.

Lansky, M. R. (2005). Hidden shame. *J. Am. Psychoanal. Assoc.*, 53(3), 865–890.

Lansky, M. R. & Morrison, A. P. (Eds.). (1997). *The Widening Scope of Shame.* Hillsdale, NJ: The Analytic Press.

Laplanche, J. (1987). *New Foundations for Psychoanalysis.* Oxford: Basil Blackwell.

Laplanche, J. (2004). Die rätselhaften Botschaften des anderen und ihre Konsequenzen für den Begriff des 'Unbewußten' im Rahmen der Allgemeinen Verführungstheorie. *Psyche – Z. Psychoanal.*, 58, 898–913.

Laub, D. (2000). Eros oder Thanatos? Der Kampf um die Erzählbarkeit des Traumas. *Psyche – Z. Psychoanal.*, 54, 860–894.

Laub, D. & Auerhahn, N. C. (1993). Knowing and not knowing massive psychic trauma: forms of traumatic memory. *Int. J. Psycho-Anal.*, 74(2), 287–302.

Laub, D. & Lee, S. (2003). Thanatos and massive psychic trauma: the impact of the death instinct on knowing, remembering, and forgetting. *J. Am. Psychoanal. Assoc.*, 51(2), 433–464.

Leuzinger-Bohleber, M. (2015). *Finding the Body in the Mind: Embodied Memories, Trauma and Depression.* London: Karnac.

Leuzinger-Bohleber, M. & Pfeifer, R. (2015). Trauma, Übertragung und Embodied Memories – zum Dialog zwischen Psychoanalyse und Embodied Cognitive Science, 147–180. In: Leuzinger-Bohleber, M., Böker, H., Northoff, G. & Solms, M. (Eds.). (2015) *Psychoanalyse und Neurowissenschaften: Chancen – Grenzen – Kontroversen.* Stuttgart: Kohlhammer.

Levin, S. (1967). Some metapsychological considerations on the differentiation between shame and guilt. *Int. J. Psycho-Anal.*, 48(2), 267–276.

Lévinas, E. (1978). *Otherwise than Being and Beyond Essence.* Dordrecht: Springer Science+Business Media.

Levine, H. B., Reed, G. B. & Scarfone, D. (Eds.). (2013). *Unrepresented States and the Construction of Meaning: Clinical and Theoretical Contributions.* London: Karnac.

Lewis, H. B. (1971). *Shame and Guilt in Neurosis*. New York: International Universities Press.

Lewis, H. B. (Ed.). (1987). *The Role of Shame in Symptom Formation*. Hillsdale, NJ: Analytic Press.

Lindahl, T. R. & West, S. C. (Eds.). (1995). *DNA Repair and Recombination*. London: Chapman & Hall.

Loewald, H. W. (1962a). Internalization, separation, mourning, and the superego. *Psychoanal. Q.*, 31, 483–504.

Loewald, H. W. (1962b). The superego and the ego-ideal. *Int. J. Psycho-Anal.*, 43, 264–268.

Loewald, H. W. (1980). (1989 Edition). *Papers on Psychoanalysis*. New Haven, London: Yale Universities Press.

Lombardi, R. (2007). Shame in relation to the body, sex and death: a clinical exploration of the psychotic levels of shame. *Psychoanal. Dial.*, 17(3), 385–399.

Lothane, Z. (1992). *In Defence of Schreber: Soul Murder and Psychiatry*. Hillsdale, NJ: Analytic Press.

Lynd, H. M. (1958). *On Shame and the Search for Identity*. London: Routledge & Kegan Paul.

Maurer, E. (2004). Zorn Gottes, 1390–1395. In: Ritter, H., Gründer, K. & Gabriel, G. (2004). *Historisches Wörterbuch der Philosophie, Bd. 12*. Basel: Schwabe.

McCrory, E., De Brito, S. A. & Viding, E. (2011). The impact of childhood maltreatment: a review of neurobiological and genetic factors. *Frontiers in Psychiatry*, 2(48), 1–14.

McLaughlin, J. T. (1987). The play of transference: some reflections on enactment in the psychoanalytic situation. *J. Am. Psychoanal. Assoc.*, 35(3), 557–582.

McLaughlin, J. T. (1991). Clinical and theoretical aspects of enactment. *J. Am. Psychoanal. Assoc.*, 39(3), 595–614.

Meltzer, D. (1966). The relation of anal masturbation to projective identification. *Int. J. Psycho-Anal.*, 47(2–3), 335–342.

Meltzer, D. (1968). Terror, persecution, dread – a dissection of paranoid anxieties. *Int. J. Psycho-Anal.*, 49(2), 396–401.

Meltzer, D. (1983). *Dream Life: A Re-examination of Psychoanalytical Theory and Technique*. Perthshire: Clunie Press.

Meltzer, D. (1992). *The Claustrum: An Investigation of Claustrophobic Phenomena*. Perthshire: Clunie Press.

Miller, S. (1985). *The Shame Experience*. Hillsdale, NJ: The Analytic Press.

Milton, J. (1667). *Paradise Lost: A Poem in Ten Books*. London: S. Simmons.

Money-Kyrle, R. (1956). Normale Gegenübertragung und mögliche Abweichungen, 19–36. In: Frank, C. & Weiss, H. (Eds.). (2003). *Normale Gegenübertragung und mögliche Abweichungen: Zur Aktualität von R. Money-Kyrles Verständnis des Gegenübertragungsprozesses*. Tübingen: Edition Diskord.

Money-Kyrle, R. (1962). Megalomania, 376–388. In: Meltzer, D. & O'Shaughnessy, E. (Eds.). (1978). *The Collected Papers of Roger Money-Kyrle*. Perthshire: Clunie Press.

Money-Kyrle, R. (1968). Cognitive development, 416–433. In: Meltzer, D. & O'Shaughnessy, E. (Eds.). (1978). *The Collected Papers of Roger Money-Kyrle*. Perthshire: Clunie Press.

Money-Kyrle, R. (1971). The aim of psychoanalysis. *Int. J. Psycho-Anal.*, 52, 103–106.

Morrison, A. P. (1983). Shame, ideal self, and narcissism. *Contemporary Psychoanalysis*, 19(2), 295–318.

Morrison, A. P. (1989). *Shame: The Underside of Narcissism*. New York, London: The Analytic Press.

Morus, T. (1516). (1965 Edition). Libellus vere aureus nec minus salutaris quam festivus de optimo rei publicae statu, deque nova Insula Utopia. *Yale Edition of the Complete Works of Thomas More, Vol. 4*. New Haven, London: Yale University Press.

Nathanson, D. L. (Ed.). (1987). *The Many Faces of Shame*. New York: Guilford Press.

Niederland, W. G. (1959a). Schreber: father and son. *Psychoanal. Q.*, 28(2), 151–169.

Niederland, W. G. (1959b). The 'miracled-up' world of Schreber's childhood. *Psychoanal. St. Child*, 14(1), 383–413.

Nunberg, H. G. (1920). On the catatonic attack, 3–23. In: Nunberg, H. G. (1948). *Practice and Theory of Psychoanalysis, Vol. 1*. New York: International Universities Press.

Nunberg, H. G. (1926). The sense of guilt and the need for punishment, 89–101. In: Nunberg, H. G. (1948). *Practice and Theory of Psychoanalysis, Vol. 1*. New York: International Universities Press.

Nunberg, H. G. (1931). The synthetic function of the ego, 120–136. In: Nunberg, H. G. (1948). *Practice and Theory of Psychoanalysis, Vol. 1*. New York: International Universities Press.

Nunberg, H. G. (1932). Psychoanalyse des Schamgefühls. *Psychoanalytische Bewegung*, 4(6), 505–507.

Ornstein, A. (1981). The aging survivor of the Holocaust. The effects of the Holocaust on life-cycle experiences: the creation and re-creation of families. *J. Geriatr. Psychiatry*, 14(2), 135–154.

Ornstein, A. (1985). Survival and recovery. *Psychoanal. Inq.*, 5(1), 99–130.

O'Shaughnessy, E. (1981). A clinical study of a defensive organization. *Int. J. Psycho-Anal.*, 62(3), 359–369.

O'Shaughnessy, E. (1989). Ways of seeing: 3. Seeing with meaning and emotion. *J. Child Psychother.*, 15(2), 27–31.

O'Shaughnessy, E. (1992). Enclaves and excursions. *Int. J. Psycho-Anal.*, 73(4), 603–611.

O'Shaughnessy, E. (1999). Relating to the superego. *Int. J. Psycho-Anal.*, 80(5), 861–870.

O'Shaughnessy, E. (2008). On gratitude, 79–91. In: Roth, P. & Lemma, A. (Eds.). (2008). *Envy and Gratitude Revisited*. London: International Psychoanalytic Association.

Ostendorf, U. (2012). Repair oder Reparation? Bewegungen zwischen trügerischer Hoffnung und realistischer Veränderung. *Jahrb. Psychoanal.*, 65, 37–58.

Özbek, T. (2015). Trauma und Reparation: Koreferat zum Vortrag von Heinz Weiss, 109–118. In: Allert, A., Rühling, K., Zwiebel & R. (Eds.). (2015). *Pluralität und Singularität in der Psychoanalyse, Tagungsband, Frühjahrstagung der Deutschen Psychoanalytischen Vereinigung.* Kassel, Gießen: Psychosozial-Verlag.

Piers, G. & Singer, M. B. (1953). *Shame and Guilt: A Psychoanalytic and a Cultural Study.* Springfield: Charles C. Thomas.

Potten, C. & Wilson, J. (2004). *Apoptosis. The Life and Death of Cells.* Cambridge, New York, Melbourne, Madrid, Cape Town: Cambridge University Press.

Potter, B. (2015). *Elements of Reparation, Truth, Faith, and Transformation in the Works of Heidegger, Bion and Beyond.* London: Karnac.

Rakoczy, T. (1996). *Böser Blick, Macht des Auges und Neid der Götter: Classica Monacensia 13.* Tübingen: Gunter Narr Verlag.

Reiner, H. (1972). Dankbarkeit, 9–11. In: Ritter, H. (Ed.). (1972). *Historisches Wörterbuch der Philosophie, Vol. 2.* Basel: Schwabe.

Rey, J. H. (1979). Schizoide Phänomene im Borderline-Syndrom, 253–287. In: Bott Spillius, E. (Ed.). (2016). *Melanie Klein Heute. Entwicklungen in Theorie und Praxis, Bd. 1, 5. Aufl.* Stuttgart: Klett-Cotta.

Rey, J. H. (1986). Reparation. *Journal of the Melanie Klein Society,* 4, 5–35.

Rey, H. (1988). That which patients bring to analysis. *Int. J. Psycho-Anal.*, 69, 457–470.

Rey, H. (1994). *Universals of Psychoanalysis in the Treatment of Psychotic and Borderline States.* London: Free Association.

Ricoeur, P. (1998). (2004 Edition). *Das Rätsel der Vergangenheit. Erinnern – Vergessen – Verzeihen, 4. Aufl.* Göttingen: Wallstein.

Ricoeur, P. (2004). *Memory, History, Forgetting.* Chicago: Chicago University Press.

Riesenberg-Malcolm, R. (1970). The mirror: a perverse sexual phantasy in a woman seen as a defence against psychotic breakdown, 15–37. In: Riesenberg-Malcolm, R. & Roth, P. (Ed.). (1999). *On Bearing Unbearable States of Mind.* London, New York: Routledge.

Riesenberg-Malcolm, R. (1981). Self-punishment as defence, 93–112. In: Riesenberg-Malcolm, R. & Roth, P. (Ed.). (1999). *On Bearing Unbearable States of Mind.* London, New York: Routledge.

Riesenberg-Malcolm, R. (1986). Interpretation: the past in the present. *Int. R. Psycho-Anal.*, 13(4), 433–443.

Riesenberg-Malcolm, R. (1987). The constitution and operation of the super ego. *Psychoanal. Psychother.*, 3(2), 149–159.

Riesenberg-Malcolm, R. (1990). As-if: the phenomenon of not learning. *Int. J. Psycho-Anal.*, 71(3), 385–392.

Riesenberg-Malcolm, R. (1999). Two ways of experiencing shame. Unpublished lecture, 41th IPA Congress, Santiago de Chile.

Riesenberg-Malcolm, R. (2004). Bedeutsames Vergessen: Eine klinische Untersuchung. *Jahrb. Psychoanal.*, 48, 9–26.

Riesenberg-Malcolm, R. & Roth, P. (Ed.). (1999). *On Bearing Unbearable States of Mind.* London, New York: Routledge.

Rinofner-Kreidl, S. (2012). Scham und Autonomie, 163–191. In: Lembeck, K.-H., Mertens, K. & Orth, E. W. (Eds.). (2012). *Phänomenologische Forschungen 2012.* Hamburg: Felix Meiner Verlag GmbH.

Rivière, J. (1936). A contribution to the analysis of the negative therapeutic reaction. *Int. J. Psycho-Anal.*, 17, 304–320.

Rizzuto, A. M. (1991). Shame in psychoanalysis: the function in unconscious fantasies. *Int. J. Psycho-Anal.*, 72(2), 297–312.

Rosenfeld, H. A. (1950). Note on the psychopathology of confusional states in chronic schizophrenias. *Int. J. Psycho-Anal.*, 31, 132–137.

Rosenfeld, H. A. (1964a). The psychopathology of hypochondriasis, 180–199. In: Rosenfeld, H. A. (1965). *Psychotic States: A Psychoanalytical Approach.* London: The Hogarth Press.

Rosenfeld, H. A. (1964b). An investigation into the need of neurotic and psychotic patients to act out during analysis, 200–216. In: Rosenfeld, H. A. (1965). *Psychotic States: A Psychoanalytical Approach.* London: The Hogarth Press.

Rosenfeld, H. A. (1965). *Psychotic States: A Psychoanalytical Approach.* London: The Hogarth Press.

Rosenfeld, H. A. (1971). A clinical approach to the psychoanalytic theory of the life and death instincts: an investigation into the aggressive aspects of narcissism. *Int. J. Psycho-Anal.*, 52(2), 169–178.

Rosenfeld, H. A. (1978). Notes on the psychopathology and psychoanalytic treatment of some borderline patients. *Int. J. Psycho-Anal.*, 59(2–3), 215–221.

Rosenfeld, H. A. (1987). *Impasse and Interpretation: Therapeutic and Antitherapeutic Factors in the Psychoanalytic Treatment of Psychotic, Borderline, and Neurotic Patients.* London: Tavistock Publications.

Rosenfeld, H. A. (2001). *The Italian Seminars.* London: Karnac.

Ross, W. D. (Ed.). (1925). *Aristotle: The Nikomachean Ethics.* Oxford: Oxford University Press.

Ross, W. D. (Ed.). (1959). *Aristotle: Ars Rhetorica.* Oxford: Oxford University Press.

Roth, P. & Lemma, A. (Eds.). (2008). *Envy and Gratitude Revisited.* London: International Psychoanalytic Association.

Rothstein, A. M. (1994). Shame and the superego: clinical and theoretical considerations. *Psychoanal. St. Child*, 49, 263–277.

Rusbridger, R. (2011). Narzissmus und Grandiosität bei König Lear. Unpublished lecture. Stuttgart, 22th October 2011.

Ryan, J. K. (Transl.). (1960). *The Confessions of Saint Augustine.* New York: Image Books.

Sandler, J. (1976). Gegenübertragung und Bereitschaft zur Rollenübernahme. *Psyche – Z. Psychoanal.*, 30(4), 297–305.

Sartre, J.-P. (1943). (2010 Edition). *Being and Nothingness: An Essay on Phenomenological Ontology.* Abingdon, New York: Routledge.

Sas, S. A. (1992). Ambiguity as the route to shame. *Int. J. Psycho-Anal.*, 73(2), 329–341.

Scheler, M. (1915). Das Ressentiment im Aufbau der Moralen, 33–147. In: Scheler, M. (1955). *Gesammelte Werke, Bd. 3.* Bern: Francke.

Schmahl, C., Bohus, M., Esposito, F., Treede, R. D., Di Salle, F., Greffrath, W., Ludaescher, P., Jochims, A., Lieb, K., Scheffler, K., Hennig, J. & Seifritz, E. (2006). Neural correlates of antinociception in borderline personality disorder. *Arch. Gen. Psychiatry*, 63(6), 659–667.

Schmithüsen, G. (2004). 'Die Zeit steht still in rasender Eile'. Eine psychoanalytische Einzelfallstudie zu frühem Trauma und Zeiterleben. *Psyche – Z. Psychoanal.*, 58(4), 293–320.

Schöpf, A. (2005). *Die Wiederkehr der Rache: Eine Hermeneutik der Macht.* Würzburg: Königshausen & Neumann.

Schore, A. N. (1991). Early superego development: the emergence of shame and narcissistic affect regulation in the practicing period. *Psychoanal. Contemp. Thought*, 14(2), 187–250.

Schore, A. N. (2001). Effects of a secure attachment relationship on right brain development, affect regulation, and infant mental health. *Infant Mental Health Journal*, 22(1–2), 7–66.

Schreber, D. P. (1903). (1955 Edition). *Memoirs of my Nervous Illness.* London: Dawson.

Sebald, W. G. (1997). *The Emigrants.* London: The Harvill Press.

Sebald, W. G. (1999). *The Rings of Saturn.* London: The Harvill Press.

Sebald, W. G. (2001). *Austerlitz.* London: Penguin Books.

Segal, H. (1952). A psycho-analytical approach to aesthetics. *Int. J. Psycho-Anal.*, 33, 196–207.

Segal, H. (1957). Notes on symbol formation. *Int. J. Psycho-Anal.*, 38, 391–397.

Segal, H. (1964). *Melanie Klein: An Introduction to her Work.* London: Hogarth Press.

Segal, H. (1978). On symbolism. *Int. J. Psycho-Anal.*, 59(2–3), 315–319.

Segal, H. (1981). (1991 Edition). *Wahnvorstellung und künstlerische Kreativität.* Stuttgart: Klett-Cotta.

Segal, H. (1991). *Dream Phantasy and Art.* London, New York: Routledge.

Segal, H. (1997a). The uses and abuses of counter-transference, 111–119. In: Segal, H. & Abel-Hirsch, N. (Ed.). (1997). *Psychoanalysis, Literature and War: Papers 1972–1995.* London, New York: Routledge.

Segal, H. (1997b). The Oedipus complex today, 86–94. In: Segal, H. & Abel-Hirsch, N. v. (Ed.). (1997). *Psychoanalysis, Literature and War: Papers 1972–1995.* London, New York: Routledge.

Segal, H. (1999). Ödipuskomplex und Symbolisierung, 48–61. In: Weiss, H. (Ed.). (1999). *Ödipuskomplex und Symbolbildung. Ihre Bedeutung bei Borderline-Zuständen und frühen Störungen.* Tübingen: Edition Diskord.

Segal, H. (2007). Vision, 61–68. In: Segal, H. & Abel-Hirsch, N. v. (Ed.). (2007). *Today, Yesterday and Tomorrow.* London, New York: Routledge.

Seidler, G. H. (1995). *Der Blick des Anderen: Eine Analyse der Scham*. (4th Edition, 2015). Stuttgart: Klett-Cotta.

Seneca (1928 Edition). *De Ira. On Anger. Moral Essays*. London: Heinemann.

Shengold, L. L. (1979). Child abuse and deprivation: soul murder. *J. Am. Psychoanal. Assoc.*, 27(3), 533–559.

Simons, L. E., Moulton, E. A., Linnman, C., Carpino, E., Becerra, L. & Borsook, D. (2014). The human amygdala and pain: evidence from neuroimaging. *Human Brain Mapping*, 35(2), 527–538.

Sodré, I. (1994). Obsessional certainty versus obsessional doubt: from two to three. *Psychoanal. Inq.*, 14(3), 379–392.

Southwick, S. M. & Charney, D. S. (2012). *Resilience: The Science of Mastery.* Cambridge, New York, Cape Town, Singapore, São Paulo, Delhi, Mexico City: Cambridge University Press.

Spero, M. H. (1984). Shame: an object-relational formulation. *Psychoanal. St. Child*, 39, 259–282.

Spielrein, S. (1920). Das Schamgefühl bei Kindern. *Int. Zschr. f. Psychoanal.*, 6, 157–158.

Spillius, E., Milton, J., Garvey, P., Couve, C. & Steiner, D. (2011). *The New Dictionary of Kleinian Thought*. London, New York: Routledge.

Spillius, E. & O'Shaughnessy, E. (Eds.). (2012). *Projective Identification: The Fate of a Concept*. London, New York: Routledge.

Steinberg, B. S. (1991). Psychoanalytic concepts in international politics: the role of shame and humiliation. *Int. J. Psycho-Anal.*, 18(1), 65–85.

Steiner, J. (1985). Turning a blind eye: The cover-up for Oedipus. *Int. Rev. Psycho-Anal.*, 12, 161–172.

Steiner, J. (1987). The interplay between pathological organizations and the paranoid-schizoid and depressive positions. *Int. J. Psycho-Anal.*, 68(1), 69–80.

Steiner, J. (1990). The retreat from truth to omnipotence in Sophocles' Oedipus at Colonus. *Int. Rev. Psycho-Anal.*, 17(2), 227–237.

Steiner, J. (1993). *Psychic Retreats: Pathological organisations in Psychotic, Neurotic and Borderline Patients*. London, New York: Routledge.

Steiner, J. (1996). Revenge and resentment in the 'Oedipus Situation'. *Int. J. Psycho-Anal.*, 77(3), 433–443.

Steiner, J. (2002). Fortschritte in einer Analyse, Verlegenheit und Empörung, 67–88. In: Weiss, H. & Frank, C. (Eds.). (2002). *Pathologische Persönlichkeitsorganisationen als Abwehr psychischer Veränderung*. Tübingen: Edition Diskord.

Steiner, J. (2004). Gaze, dominance and humiliation in the Schreber case. *Int. J. Psycho-Anal.*, 85(2), 269–284.

Steiner, J. (2006a). (4th Edition, 2015, Eds. Weiss, H. & Frank, C.). *Narzisstische Einbrüche: Sehen und Gesehenwerden. Scham und Verlegenheit bei pathologischen Persönlichkeitsorganisationen*. Stuttgart: Klett-Cotta.

Steiner, J. (2006b). Interpretative enactments and the analytic setting. *Int. J. Psycho-Anal.*, 87(2), 315–320.

Steiner, J. (2011a). *Seeing an Being Seen: Emerging from a Psychic Retreat*. London, New York: Routledge.

Steiner, J. (2011b). The numbing feeling of reality. *Psychoanal. Q.*, 80(1), 73–89.

Steiner, J. (2011c). Helplessness and the exercise of power in the analytic session. *Int. J. Psycho-Anal.*, 92(1), 135–147.

Steiner, J. (2014). (Eds. Weiss, H. & Frank, C.). *Seelische Rückzugsorte verlassen: Therapeutische Schritte zur Aufgabe der Borderline-Position*. Stuttgart: Klett-Cotta.

Steiner, J. (2015). Seeing and being seen: shame in the clinical situation. *Int. J. Psycho-Anal.*, 96(6), 1589–1601.

Steiner, J. (Ed.). (2017). *Melanie Klein's Unpublished Lectures on Technique: Their Relevance for Contemporary Psychoanalysis*. London, New York: Routledge.

Steiner, J. (2018). The trauma and disillusionment of Oedipus. *Int. J. Psycho-Anal.*, 99(3), 1–14.

Stern, D. (1985). *The Interpersonal World of the Infant*. New York: Basic Books.

Strachey, J. (1934). The nature of the therapeutic action of psycho-analysis. *Int. J. Psycho-Anal.*, 15, 127–159.

Straus, E. (1930). *Geschehnis und Erlebnis – eine historiologische Deutung des psychischen Traumas und der Renten-Neurose*. Berlin: Springer.

Teicher, M. H., Andersen, S. L., Polcari, A., Anderson, C. M., Navalta, C. P. & Kim, D. M. (2003). The neurobiological consequences of early stress and childhood maltreatment. *Neuroscience and Biobehavioral Reviews*, 27(1–2), 33–44.

Teising, M. (2005). Permeability and demarcation in the psychoanalytic process: functions of the contact-barrier. *Int. J. Psycho-Anal.*, 86(6), 1627–1644.

Teising, M. (2015). Koreferat zu Heinz Weiss: 'Gedanken über Trauma, Wiedergutmachung und die Grenzen von Wiedergutmachung bei schwer traumatisierten Patienten. Eine klinische Untersuchung', 102–108. In: Allert, A., Rühling, K. & Zwiebel, R. (Eds.). (2015). *Pluralität und Singularität in der Psychoanalyse, Tagungsband, Frühjahrstagung der Deutschen Psychoanalytischen Vereinigung*. Kassel, Gießen: Psychosozial-Verlag.

Thrane, G. (1979). Shame and the construction of the self. *Ann. Psychoanal.*, 7, 321–341.

van der Kolk, B. A. (2003). The neurobiology of childhood trauma and abuse. *Child Adolesc. Psychiatric. Clin. N. Am.*, 12(2), 293–317.

Walde, C. (2004). Zorn, 1382–1385. In: Ritter, H., Gründer, K. & Gabriel, G. (2004). *Historisches Wörterbuch der Philosophie, Bd. 12*. Basel: Schwabe.

Wehkamp, J. & Stange, E. F. (2015). Angeborene Immunität und Schleimhautbarriere, 24–39. In: Stange, E. F. (Ed.). (2015). *Entzündliche Darmerkrankungen: Klinik, Diagnostik und Therapie*. Stuttgart: Schattauer.

Weiss, H. (1988). *Der Andere in der Übertragung: Untersuchung über die analytische Situation und die Intersubjektivität in der Psychoanalyse*. Stuttgart, Bad Cannstatt: fromann-holzboog.

Weiss, H. (2003). Verstehen als Wiedergutmachung – Deutung als Reprojektion. Zur Aktualität von R. Money-Kyrles Verständnis der Gegenübertragung als Transformationsprozeß, 158–173. In: Frank, C. & Weiss, H.

(Eds.). (2003). *Normale Gegenübertragung und mögliche Abweichungen. Zur Aktualität von R. Money-Kyrles Verständnis des Gegenübertragungsprozesses.* Tübingen: Edition Diskord.

Weiss, H. (2005). Wenn das Geschehene erst dann geschieht, wenn wir es denken können – Überlegungen zur Konstruktion des inneren Raumes und zur zeitlichen Rekonstruktion. *Psyche – Z. Psychoanal.*, 59(Beiheft), 65–77.

Weiss, H. (2008). Groll, Scham und Zorn. Überlegungen zur Differenzierung narzisstischer Zustände. *Psyche – Z. Psychoanal.*, 62, 866–886.

Weiss, H. (2009). *Das Labyrinth der Borderline-Kommunikation: Klinische Zugänge zum Erleben von Raum und Zeit.* Stuttgart: Klett-Cotta.

Weiss, H. (2012a). Utopien und Dystopien als Orte des seelischen Rückzugs. *Psyche – Z. Psychoanal.*, 66(4), 310–330.

Weiss, H. (2012b). Wiedergutmachung beim Borderline-Patienten. *Jahrb. Psychoanal.*, 65, 59–80.

Weiss, H. (2013). The explosion of the present and the encapsulation of time: transference phenomena in the analysis of a psychotic patient. *Int. J. Psycho-Anal.*, 94(6), 1057–1075.

Weiss, H. (2014a). Eine Reinterpretation von Susan Isaacs: The Nature and Function of Phantasy, 273–282. In: Paul, R. et al. (Eds.). (2014). *Passagen, Transformationen – Neugier und Trauer in Prozessen der Veränderung. Tagungsband der Herbsttagung der Deutschen Psychoanalytischen Vereinigung.* Bad Homburg: Deutsche Psychoanalytische Vereinigung.

Weiss, H. (2014b). 'Aller Tage Abend' – Anmerkungen zu Jenny Erpenbecks Roman über das Rätsel der Zeit. *Psyche – Z. Psychoanal.*, 68(8), 704–712.

Weiss, H. (2015a). Three papers on splitting: a brief introduction. *Int. J. Psycho-Anal.*, 96(1), 119–122.

Weiss, H. (2015b). Überlegungen zum agora-klaustrophoben Dilemma des Borderline-Patienten. *Psyche – Z. Psychoanal.*, 69, 916–935.

Weiss, H. (2015c). Introduction: the role of shame in psychoanalytic theory and practice. *Int. J. Psycho-Anal.*, 96(6), 1585–1588.

Weiss, H. (2016). Der Turm. Über die Anziehungskraft eines Rückzugsorts. *Psyche – Z. Psychoanal.*, 70, 134–153.

Weiss, H. & Frank, C. (1996). Rekonstruktion des Würzburger Falles 'Erna' von Melanie Klein. Seine Bedeutung für die Entwicklung von Kleins theoretischen Konzepten am Übergang zwischen ihren Berliner und Londoner Jahren, 126–143. In: Weiss, H. & Lang, H. (Eds.). (1996). *Psychoanalyse heute und vor 70 Jahren: Zur Erinnerung an die 1. Deutsche Zusammenkunft für Psychoanalyse am 11. und 12. Oktober 1924 in Würzburg.* Tübingen: Edition Diskord.

Weiss, H. & Frank, C. (Eds.). (2002). *Pathologische Persönlichkeitsorganisationen als Abwehr psychischer Veränderung.* Tübingen: Edition Diskord.

Weiss, H. & Pagel, G. (1995). Sprache, Gefühl und Denken – oder: Wie psychische Bedeutungen entstehen. Eine Auseinandersetzung mit den Theorien W. R. Bions und J. Lacans. *Jahrb. Psychoanal.*, 34, 142–178.

Weiss, L. (2016). Hegel, Freud und der Begriff der Erinnerung, 225–240. In: Lang, H., Dybel, P. & Pagel, G. (Eds.). (2016). *Hermeneutik und Psychoanalyse: Perspektiven und Kontroversen.* Würzburg: Königshausen & Neumann.

Williams, G. (1997). *Internal Landscapes and Foreign Bodies: Eating Disorders and Other Pathologies.* London: Duckworth.

Winnicott, D. W. (1935). The manic defence, 129–144. In: Winnicott, D. W. (1975). *Through Paediatrics to Psycho-Analysis.* London: The Hogarth Press.

Winnicott, D. W. (1960a). The theory of the parent-infant relationship. *Int. J. Psycho-Anal.,* 41, 585–595.

Winnicott, D. W. (1960b). Ego distortion in terms of true and false self, 140–152. In: Winnicott, D. W. (1965). *The Maturational Processes and the Facilitating Environment: Studies in the Theory of Emotional Development.* London: The Hogarth Press.

Winnicott, D. W. (1964). Postscriptum to: Classification: Is there a psychoanalytic contribution to psychiatric classification?, 139. In: Winnicott, D. W. (1965). *The Maturational Processes and the Facilitating Environment: Studies in the Theory of Emotional Development.* London: The Hogarth Press.

Winnicott, D. W. (1967). The mirror-role of mother and family in child development. In: Winnicott, D. W. (1971). *Playing and Reality.* London: Tavistock Publications.

Winnicott, D. W. (1971). *Playing and Reality.* London: Tavistock Publications.

Wurmser, L. (1981). *The Mask of Shame.* London: John Hopkins University Press.

Wurmser, L. (1987). (3rd Edition, 2000). *Flucht vor dem Gewissen: Analyse von Über-Ich und Abwehr bei schweren Neurosen.* Göttingen: Vandenhoeck & Ruprecht.

Wurmser, L. (1991). *Scham und der böse Blick: Verstehen der negativen therapeutischen Reaktion.* Stuttgart: Kohlhammer.

Wurmser, L. (2003). The annihilating power of absoluteness: superego analysis in the severe neuroses, especially in character perversion. *Psychoanal. Psychol.,* 20(2), 214–235.

Wurmser, L. (2004). Psychoanalytic reflections on 9/11, terrorism, and genocidal prejudice: roots and sequels. *J. Am. Psychoanal. Assoc.,* 52(3), 911–926.

Wurmser, L. (2015). Primary shame, mortal wound and tragic circularity: some new reflections on shame and shame conflicts. *Int. J. Psycho-Anal.,* 96(6), 1615–1634.

Zahavi, D. (2013). Scham als soziales Gefühl, 319–337. In: Fonfara, D., Lembeck, K.-H., Lohmar, D., Mertens, K. & OrthE. W. (Eds.). (2013). *Phänomenologische Forschungen 2013.* Hamburg: Felix Meiner Verlag GmbH.

Index

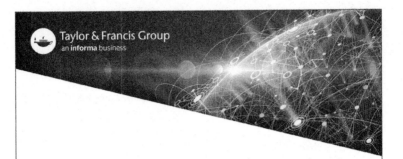